ADVANCE PRAISE

"I doubt anybody has ever described Widmer brothers Kurt and Rob as punk. After all, one of Kurt's favorite words is charming. But in this book, Jeff Alworth offers us the story of two brothers who never abandoned the DIY ethos of the 1980s as they guided their new wave brewery into the mainstream."

—Stan Hieronymus, *Appellation Beer*

"Jeff Alworth and the Widmers team up to tell one of the most important, instructive, and inspiring stories in craft beer. In Jeff's hands, the Widmers' story is deftly told, a must-read for beer fans in Portland and well beyond."

—Josh Noel, author of *Barrel-Aged Stout and Selling Out: Goose Island, Anheuser-Busch, and How Craft Beer Became Big Business*

"Jeff Alworth presents an entertaining and illuminating story that explores how Kurt and Rob Widmer, middle-class boys from Portland, defied the odds to create one of the most successful craft beer brands in the country. Along the way, they helped launch craft beer in Oregon and the concept of Portland as Beervana. The book is packed with personal anecdotes from the Widmers and others who were involved in or watched their story unfold. Required reading for fans of craft beer, in Oregon and beyond."

—Pete Dunlop, *Portland Beer: Crafting the Road to Beervana*

"Jeff Alworth's *The Widmer Way* is essential reading for any Portlander. It carries a personalized approach to the background of modern craft brewing in Oregon, a dramatically changing landscape over the last thirty years. Alworth encapsulates the Widmers' story in the way he does best, with a plethora of easily digestible facts about the marriage of beer and Portland culture."

—Holly Amlin, *PDXBeerGirl*

"*The Widmer Way* tells the story of two brothers' rise to craft beer stardom in the face of seemingly insurmountable odds. Rob and Kurt Widmer had no existing small brewery business model to follow, yet through grit and determination, they built a brewery and led it to the top of a newly established industry. Alworth's telling of the Widmer Brothers prodigious rise is informative and inspirational, showing what is possible when human passion supersedes what is probable and feasible."

—Bryan Carey, *Great Beer Now*

"This is a tale of two brothers, with beer-making, German genes behind them and major financial headwinds in front of them, risking it all to create a brewing legacy that today has helped shape the Pacific Northwest. Rob and Kurt Widmer were born and grew up in Portland in the 1950s. Had they been from somewhere else, the town affectionately known as 'Beervana' might have another nickname today. But above all, the story that Jeff Alworth has artfully penned is an inspirational testament to hard work and persistence, two traits that served the brothers well and remain elements of the 'Widmer Way,' a philosophy that still guides them to this day."

—Larry Hawthorne, *The Beer Drinker's Guide to Munich*

"A thoughtful, and loving, rumination on a company, its people, and the city they call home."

—Maureen Ogle, *Ambitious Brew: The Story of American Beer*

"Anyone interested in the history of American craft brewing owes it to themselves to check out Jeff Alworth's latest book, *The Widmer Way*. It does a masterful job of exploring the tremendous impact that Kurt and Rob have had on beer and brewing since 1985."

—Bill Howell, *Beer on the Last Frontier: The Craft Breweries of Alaska*; *Alaska Beer: Liquid Gold in the Land of the Midnight Sun*

THE WIDMER WAY

HOW TWO BROTHERS LED PORTLAND'S CRAFT BEER REVOLUTION

THE WIDMER WAY

HOW TWO BROTHERS LED
PORTLAND'S CRAFT BEER REVOLUTION

JEFF ALWORTH

OOLIGAN PRESS | PORTLAND, OR

Ooligan Press
Portland State University
Post Office Box 751, Portland, Oregon 97207
503-725-9748
ooligan@ooliganpress.pdx.edu
http://ooligan.pdx.edu

Library of Congress Cataloging-in-Publication Data
Names: Alworth, Jeff, author.
Title: The Widmer way: how two brothers led Portland's craft beer revolution/Jeff Alworth.
Description: Portland, Oregon: Ooligan Press, [2019]
Identifiers: LCCN 2018041512 (print) | LCCN 2018042420 (ebook) | ISBN 9781947845039 (ebook) | ISBN 9781947845022 (pbk.)
Subjects: LCSH: Widmer Brothers Brewing. | Beer industry—Oregon—Portland. | Microbreweries—Oregon—Portland.
Classification: LCC HD9397.U54 (ebook) | LCC HD9397.U54 W5335 2019 (print) | DDC 338.7/6634209795—dc23

Cover design by Jenny Kimura
Interior design by Jenny Kimura and Hanna Ziegler

References to website URLs were accurate at the time of writing. Neither the author nor Ooligan Press is responsible for URLs that have changed or expired since the manuscript was prepared.

Printed in the United States of America

THE WIDMER WAY

HOW TWO BROTHERS LED PORTLAND'S
CRAFT BEER REVOLUTION

TABLE OF CONTENTS

Kurt and Rob at the Russell Street brewery, 1995.

PROLOGUE

EVERYTHING IS OBVIOUS IN RETROSPECT. EVENTS form an orderly line and lead to an inevitable conclusion. The explosion of craft brewing that has delivered over seven thousand breweries to the United States makes sense because, looking back, we filter out the conflicting or extraneous information that might have confused us in the moment. That Oregon would become the national leader in brewing; that it would have five of the forty largest breweries, the most craft beer consumption (by far), hop fields, a USDA hops research facility, two major commercial yeast labs, a burgeoning flock of malthouses; that good beer could be found in movie theaters, bowling alleys, gas stations, and alongside wine lists in the finest restaurants; that pairs of elderly women sipping stouts and tables of families with children would be familiar sights in bars—all of this makes sense to our modern minds.

And, for anyone who has a passing familiarity with local Portland history, equally unsurprising is the success of Widmer Brothers, Oregon's most prominent brewery and one of the largest in the country. It has been this way for decades, buoyed by the Northwest's first smash success, Hefeweizen, one of the most popular American beers and one that had a lot to do with launching the state's love of beer in the first place. For those of us who were old enough to remember, Widmer was the first craft brewery to find its way into bars and restaurants. It was an early trailblazer that never looked back. For those of us who were younger and grew up with Widmer, it has always been the old reliable, the city brewery. No matter what our experience, Widmer seems like it was always destined to become the brewery it is.

But around 1980, when the older of the two Widmer brothers was first turning the idea of a brewery over in his mind, none of this reality was even imaginable. The United States had just ninety breweries—a number that had fallen every year for a century. Nevertheless, Americans were drinking more beer than at any time in history, which didn't seem to indicate consumers were clamoring for more choice. When the founders of BridgePort, a contemporary of Widmer Brothers, went looking for financing, a bank loan officer laughed and told them, "Breweries don't open; they close," before rejecting their request for a loan.

Once small breweries demonstrated they had a successful business model, banks, malt and hop companies, and steel fabricators were happy to accommodate them. Now it's easy to find manufacturers happy to fabricate a brewery as small as you want it; in the 1980s, manufacturers only knew how to make gigantic breweries.

Now you can buy micro-volumes of malt, but in the 1980s, malthouses shipped product by the railcar. Now we casually talk about saisons, IPAs, and imperial stouts, but back then most drinkers had no idea there was more to beer than "regular" and "light."

To appreciate the story of Rob and Kurt Widmer, we need to tell it again, forgetting what we know about the present, and see how unlikely this "inevitable" outcome would have seemed to these young men nearly four decades ago. Even more importantly, in retelling this story, we need to pause and consider how pivotal certain decisions became in shaping their own brewery and an industry they were helping create. Craft brewing wasn't inevitable, nor was the form it took. We got here because the pioneers built it from the ground up.

I started covering the Widmer story in 1997, thirteen years after it began, as a young writer for *Willamette Week*, Portland's alt-weekly. I'd been living in Portland a little more than a decade and had gotten to know the brewery as beer fans do—pint by pint. In fact, one of my most formative experiences as a writer came at the hands of Kurt and Rob.

One year, around 1998, Widmer Brothers released a seasonal kölsch, a kind of pale ale that comes from Cologne, Germany. Breweries didn't release the volumes of beer they do now, and it was possible not just to keep track of new releases, but review them in the newspaper. I gave the beer a middling review—certainly not a negative one. Nevertheless, the next year when they rereleased the beer, I got an invitation from the brewery to have lunch with Rob and Kurt. I knew exactly what was on their minds, and braced myself for a hard sell. It never came. We had a very pleasant lunch—the topic of Widmer Kölsch never came up—but as I was leaving, they handed me a packet of very detailed information about the style's origin, brewing techniques, and tasting notes. It was the most understated effort to shift my perspective I've ever gotten, and it told me a lot about their approach.

In the two decades since then, I've continued to cover Oregon craft beer, and I started writing books in 2012. I've learned a lot about beer since the brothers sat me down and educated me about German ales. (I managed to make it to Cologne and tour a brewery there, and I shudder to think of what I wrote back in '98.) Many, many of those figures I first wrote about—and more than just a few of the breweries—have moved on. Throughout that time, Rob and Kurt have been a constant, stabilizing presence in craft beer.

When I came to this project, I knew the broad contours of the Widmer Brothers story. What I didn't know as well were the minds of the men behind it. Although Kurt and Rob have been a part of craft brewing since the moment it was born, they've managed to stand behind the crowds, away from the spotlights. Even over the course of this project, they remained reserved. Sitting down with a biographer to discuss a lifetime's success is the moment to take a victory lap, the moment to brag a little. We had four one- to two-hour sessions together, and another when they led me on a tour of the brewery. In that time, they were charming and funny, making jokes at their own expense every few minutes—and only ever approached an outright boast once. They revealed themselves not directly, but in these self-effacing jokes and the straightforward retelling of their lives.

The story you're about to read is unique. The people, the beer, and the decisions are particular to this story. But it can also be read at the level of metaphor. Each step along the way mirrors what was happening across the country, beginning with entrepreneurial pioneers starting breweries on a shoestring; their attempts to identify beer that would attract Americans used to drinking pale lager; success and expansion, and ultimately involvement with companies making the pale lagers they sought to supplant; and, in the case of Widmer Brothers, creating a new type of beer that we would come, thirty years later, to recognize as distinctly American. It is the story of Rob and Kurt Widmer; it is also the story of American craft brewing.

BEFORE THE BEGINNING

ABREWERY'S STORY DOES NOT BEGIN THE MOMENT
its founders fire up the brewhouse for the first
time. The roots of such a story plunge deeply into
the past and grow in sometimes unexpected direc-
tions. Seeds of what would later become Widmer
Brothers Brewing were planted when Rob and Kurt
were children, when their Uncle Walter took Rob
down to his cellar to sneak sips of homebrew. They
formed when Kurt took a long sojourn abroad. The
roots grew deeper when the brothers encountered
friends making their own (mostly bad) beer and
started homebrewing themselves. Keep pushing back
into the past and you discover that the story actually
began before Kurt and Rob were born, when their
grandparents, in possession of a pioneering spirit,
left their home countries to try a new life on a distant
continent. There was no single moment when the
idea of a brewery was born, complete and whole; it
evolved over time, as the different influences slowly
came together.

BORN IN PORTLAND

Rob and Kurt Widmer were born in Portland, Oregon, in the 1950s. They were the second and fourth of four siblings, separated by five years (Kurt is the elder), and the sons of Ray and Ann Widmer, the latter of whom was also a native Portlander. They grew up in East Portland and attended the now-shuttered Marshall High School before heading off to college. Kurt went to the University of Oregon, Rob to Oregon State. The brothers describe themselves entirely as creatures of Oregon, in all that entailed in the 1960s and '70s. Portland was a small city that felt like a small town, far from the forces that drove larger cities on the West Coast (and unimaginably far from points Oregonians call "back east," which may start as far west as Chicago).

Kurt graduated five years before Rob with a degree in psychology and held a series of good jobs. He spent two years in Germany working for a pharmaceutical company after graduation. He later worked for the Washington Transportation Department and was working for the Internal Revenue Service when, in 1984, he quit to work full-time on the brewery. When asked what he had in mind for a career before the brewery, he joked, "I did not have a mind before brewing. Really."

In college, Rob studied forestry and hotel and restaurant management. For Rob, an avid hiker, forestry makes sense, and restaurant management seems positively prescient for a future brewery owner, but in fact, Rob said, "I had no idea what I wanted to do after college." He rambled around the Northwest, spending time in

Montana and Washington. "I never really had much of a day job," he said, and by way of emphasizing the point mentioned that he was working as a candy maker before he returned to Portland to work more seriously on the brewery idea.

Portland is a blue-collar town, and it has always been. The earliest settlers chopped a city out of the forest and turned it into a deepwater port. It has long been the innermost reach of the Pacific Ocean, where the state's timber, grain, produce, and meat are loaded onto ships to start their seaward journeys. Well into the 1980s, it was common to see giant floats of Oregon fir pulled by tugboat down the Willamette River. As the country ramped up for world wars, steel and shipbuilding were added as major industries for the hardworking town.

Oregon has also functioned as a symbol for a better place. It beckoned Midwest farmers, who risked death to cross a continent in wagons. It was a destination for people who were equal parts dreamers, risk-takers, and hard workers. Those were the people who ended up in Portland, the same people who populated the Widmers' holiday celebrations.

It's not immediately obvious that Kurt and Rob Widmer have hearts of adventure. Outwardly, they are quiet and reserved. If you encounter them together and ask a general question about the brewery, Kurt is more likely to answer. He has an older brother's sense of authority. Yet Rob is the more social, the more likely to go to public events and interact with fans and customers.

Kurt is the kind of person who is happy to exchange pleasantries and then stand in companionable silence sipping his beer. Rob will strike up a conversation, happy to chat with anyone who offers a hand and an ear.

Rob and Kurt were swimming in the adventurous soup that was Portland, but events had to align to push them in the right direction. They grew up in a family that drank beer. One side of the family was German, the other Swiss, so the boys were raised in a culture where beer was a routine part of daily life. It seems to have been passed down through the generations.

"I always liked beer," Kurt recalled. "I can't say that when I was a little boy I really loved it, but I always wanted to taste my dad's beer—as young as six. Dad was always ready to give me a small taste." Around the Widmer house, beer was never taboo.

That the brothers' uncle, Walter, was a homebrewer was a rarity in the 1960s. Rob, in particular, remembered him fondly. "Beer was always around. Our uncle, Walter Henzi, a Swiss guy, he was a homebrewer. I remember at family dinners at their house, he would grab me and say, 'Hey, come with me,' and we would go down into their cellar to get beer. While we were down there, he would open up bottles and give me a little taste. He'd ask my opinion. He totally treated me like an adult, like he was listening to what I would say."

Henzi wasn't the only brewer in the family. The Widmers tell a legendary family story about their Great-Grandmother Engele, which may or may not have been embellished over time. That the family continued to repeat it through the decades illustrates, if nothing else, their affection for a bottle of good beer.

Great-Grandma Engele's Homebrew

KURT WIDMER: "Our great-grandmother, during the Depression, I guess, was a homebrewer—totally illegally, of course. One of her sons, our great-uncle, is pulled over for speeding in Montavilla, where they lived. He hands the cop his license and the cop says, 'Wait, you aren't Emma Engele's son, are you?' He says, 'Yes, I am,' and the cop says, 'I would trade you a non-ticket for a couple bottles of your mother's famous beer if you can make that happen.' So our great-uncle says, 'Follow me.' So that's how he beat his speeding ticket. She was a homebrewer of some renown."

Finally, one of the most formative experiences, one that not only sparked their interest in starting the brewery but acted as a font of inspiration for decades, happened five thousand miles from Portland by way of their sister. In the 1970s, the eldest Widmer daughter, Kristen, went to Germany for a year abroad. That year turned into a lifetime—she settled down, married, and has lived there ever since. After he graduated from college, Kurt packed up and joined Kristen and her husband, spending two years living in the beautiful little town of Freiburg, on the edge of the Black Forest.

The town is in the heart of the wine-growing region, and unlike many German cities that are known for their beer, it has no famous local breweries nor distinctive local beer style. But perhaps because of its understated ordinariness, Kurt was struck by how much local beer inflected daily life.

"Germany was just so charming, how beer fit into everything. Not forced in." When Kurt speaks of his time in Germany and the role he saw beer playing, he returns to the word "charming" often. "If there's a wedding, there's going to be beer; if there's a funeral, there's going to be beer. If there's a party, there's going to be beer. Where I lived, the pubs were just charming. They were all walking distance from where I lived."

German beer culture is legendary, largely for exactly the reason Kurt describes—it is a part of everything. Contrast that experience with what America had to offer in 1975. Laws governing drinking were still holdovers from the days following Prohibition; bars were often dark, windowless dens populated mainly by men. It was as if there were something disreputable about drinking beer. In Germany, the local pub was a place for families to gather. They were open and well-lit—there was nothing unseemly about them. Far from it, in fact: the only thing more common on the wall of a German pub than a stuffed deer head is a crucifix.

Looking at the close association the Widmers have with Germany, it's easy to see the connection to the years Kurt spent in Freiburg. Nevertheless, it didn't occur to him—yet—that he might try to recreate a corner of Germany back in Portland. Instead, he returned to Oregon after a two-year stay with nothing more than an appetite for better beer.

It wasn't just the Widmer household; in the late 1970s and early 1980s, the Pacific Northwest had a comparatively rich beer scene. It may seem absurd to our modern eyes to call this "diverse," but a number of regional breweries still survived—a rarity in the United States. They included Blitz-Weinhard, a venerable institution that scented downtown Portland with beer, and which introduced the notion of "premium" beer with its launch of Private Reserve.

Karl Ockert, the founding brewer at BridgePort, went to UC Davis to study brewing during this period, thinking he'd return to the area with his choice of places to brew—it was still that robust. "When I started brewing in 1983–84, Lucky Lager was still in Vancouver, Blitz was in Portland, Heidelberg had just closed down, but they were in Tacoma. Olympia was still there, Rainier was still there. So there were four or five major breweries, and then there was a malt house here [Great Western, in Vancouver, Washington], and then there were the hop growers in Yakima and Oregon. It was a very beer-centric place."

This bounty created a paradoxical situation, though; despite the relative diversity—or perhaps because of it—people were looking for better beer. That interest in better beer accelerated when, one by one, these older breweries disappeared or were snatched up by larger national beer companies. In the midst of all this, one of the most important developments at the time was homebrewing, a growing hobby that fueled the first craft breweries.

BREWING AT HOME

Independently, in entirely different states, both Rob and Kurt had started homebrewing as a way of exploring a greater range of flavors. Rob was living as a ski bum in Big Sky, Montana, when he started, apprenticing under a local who was already making his own. "I think he was kind of a weird guy, but I guess I had it in the back of my mind because of Uncle Walter, so I brewed with him," Rob said.

This was not sophisticated brewing. There's an abbreviated form of homebrewing that uses dry or liquid malt extract, which Rob remembers with a laugh. "It was just a can of extract: 'hopped ale.'" Of course, he was mail-ordering his supplies from F. H. Steinbart, a Prohibition-founded Portland homebrew store, a cornerstone of the burgeoning homebrew scene, and, later, a supplier to craft breweries.

Back in Portland, Kurt was able to visit Steinbart's in person after he caught the homebrewing bug. "A couple friends had been brewing and making *undrinkable* beer. It was horribly infected. I don't know what their motivation was, whether it was to save money or for fun, but they brewed. The beer was explosive." He stopped to tell the story of how one of these friends would dress up his girlfriend in a kind of hazmat suit and send her into the basement with tongs to pick up a bottle of homebrew. If it didn't explode, they drank it. Perversely, their incompetence inspired Kurt—still remembering the beer he'd drunk in Germany—to try his hand at it. Surely he couldn't do worse than that.

Like Rob, Kurt started out doing extract-from-a-can homebrew, but the results weren't stellar. He cobbled together a simple mash tun so he could begin using malted grain, but he was still limited by the ingredients homebrewers could buy. "The hops that were available were cheesy, old, stale hops, the yeast was freeze-dried packets—honestly, I don't know if *anyone* could have made great beer with those ingredients, but that's what was available." This foreshadowed the challenges they'd find when they scaled their production up to a commercial brewery, but at the time, he wasn't planning to go pro—just trying to make decent, interesting beer.

Kurt tends to downplay the effort and experimentation that went into this hobby at the time. But his wife, Ann, tells a slightly different story. Kurt, she said, read and thought about brewing a lot. The brewer with decades of experience may consider it small-time now, but to Ann's eyes, it was quite a production. "We had carboys and things bubbling—my kids loved it by the way, they thought it was really cool that he was brewing. We had things going all over the kitchen, things being cooked, big cookers." She describes him with his nose in books, studying as well as experimenting. The German experience was in the back of Kurt's mind, and both brothers had begun homebrewing, but the idea to start a brewery hadn't yet formed.

VISITING THE OTHER PIONEERS

Their thinking changed in the early 1980s, after they paid a visit to a curious operation in a building in Southeast Portland. Widmer Brothers and BridgePort are credited as Oregon's first craft breweries, but they weren't actually the first. That honor goes to a man named Chuck Coury, who started an ill-fated brewery called Cartwright. He brewed his first batches of beer in 1979, making Cartwright one of the very first of the new craft breweries in the United States. The beer was, unfortunately, mostly a disaster. Press accounts and internal documents of the time reveal just how little people understood about brewing or the market for beer. In an internal document, Coury wrote about his process, which included an incredibly long mashing process, an extra-long boil, and leaving the beer in the kettle overnight to cool—all practices that would cause modern brewers to gasp.

The beer was famous for having funky flavors, carbonation problems, and huge variability from batch to batch. It was nevertheless a curiosity to the homebrewers around town, who, like Rob and Kurt, were drawn to it like moths. "It was not sanitary," Kurt began, marveling. "He didn't have a wort cooler; we saw right away that he was running it into a large, open tank and just letting the ambient temperature cool it down. Overnight. Just as homebrewers without any formal education, we could see what was missing in his system. He was using an old Coca-Cola bottler for bottling. Even if the beer had gone in sanitary, I don't know if that machine was capable of doing a sanitary fill."

Most people, seeing such a place, would not think: "Hey, maybe *we* should start our own brewery," but it seems like that was when the idea started to form as a possibility. Kurt was the one who pursued the idea of a brewery first, and he and Ann did fact-finding trips to other early craft breweries. It was the oddball, cobbled-together operations that inspired him to continue—foremost, Coury's crazy system. "When I saw a brewery that was big and had lots of money, I came away *dis*couraged. When it was clearly used equipment that had been repurposed for brewing, then I was *en*couraged."

With Cartwright, Coury offered another important shaft of hope. Even though his beer was bad, retailers were excited by it. "We kept seeing that people really wanted him to succeed," Rob remembers. "They were like, 'This is so cool, opening a brewery!' People wanted him to succeed and the reason he didn't was not because it was a bad idea, but because his beer was inconsistent."

The idea for starting a brewery began to gel, and Kurt nurtured it by visiting Anchor and Sierra Nevada in California as well as Redhook and Grant's in Washington. Although some of these were well-funded endeavors ("*dis*couraging"), others showed that with some creativity and ingenuity—and a lot of elbow grease—it was possible to launch a brewery with a fairly low investment.

The brothers had reached the stage of active consideration. One model for starting a new brewery involved a large capital investment and the purchase of a proper, purpose-built brewery. A competing model replaced money with elbow grease and shiny new equipment with scavenged, secondhand vessels originally built for other purposes. The calculation came down to this: If they were going to do it, they had to do it on the cheap. And if they had to do it on the cheap, they were going to have to really work. "One thing Rob and I can do is outwork anybody," Kurt said. "We're not the smartest guys, we won't outthink anybody, but we can outwork anybody. If it comes down to that, maybe we can make a go of it."

By 1982, Rob and Kurt decided to open a brewery.

RAISING MONEY

Starting a business blind like the early craft brewers had to do was, on most accounts, a bad thing. Not only did they not know everything, they didn't know what they didn't know—and because there wasn't a craft beer market yet, there was a lot they *couldn't* know. But it did have one benefit: for the right kind of guys, that lack of knowledge granted a kind of fearlessness. After describing his homebrewing experiments and relaying their experiences seeing other breweries—particularly Cartwright—Kurt repeated something only young men in their situation would have thought. "We said: why *wouldn't* we do this?"

He would laughingly admit a few minutes later: "You know, honestly, we should have thought about that; we should have been concerned. It was really stupid what we were trying to do. No experience, no knowledge, no understanding of the basic technology or microbiology or anything. It was ridiculous." Fortunately for them, they didn't realize that—although they might have gotten an inkling as the process started to unfold.

They knew the first step was securing capital to lease space and buy equipment—money they didn't have. They began by drawing up a detailed business plan, according to which they'd need $100,000 to get started—a considerable sum for two young guys who described themselves as broke. (It's the equivalent of a quarter of a million dollars today.) They started with the banks, and quickly discovered that with their lack of experience and collateral, a loan was out of the question. Next they investigated a standard IPO, but found that they were designed for bigger launches. Instead, they discovered a version in the IRS code that was aimed at more modest businesses looking for small investments.

The Mirth of Bankers

KURT WIDMER: "We went to the five major banks in Portland. Nobody threw me out, but they would say things like, so how much brewing experience do you have? Well, we've been homebrewers for five years. Okay. And how much experience do you have running a business? Well, actually I've never run a business before. And what are you using for collateral? My '67 Datsun? It was this long list of questions a banker would logically ask."

ROB WIDMER: "It was kind of like we were speaking another language. There were no small breweries.

People thought first it was illegal and then they thought our beer would make them sick. It was like we were from another planet."

_____

This approach was perfect for the kind of fundraising they planned to do: reaching out to family and friends. It allowed a more personal appeal, and as they asked for support, they would pass out bottles of their homebrew to prospective investors as proof of concept. The way the brothers tell it now, they presented potential investors a comically dangerous plan—and they mentioned more than once that they really didn't want anyone to invest money they needed. Kurt recounted it in highly amusing terms.

"So we just put together a brochure that basically said: 'Here are the knotheads who have no clue what they're doing, they've never done this before, there's no guarantee that this is going to go anywhere, and in all likelihood the knotheads are going to go bankrupt in a matter of months. But! if you choose to invest, good luck.'"

Two of the most important investors were their sister Kristen and her husband Herbert—the sister now living in Germany. "Their investment was significantly more than any other individual—including Rob and I," Kurt said. "That was the portion that pushed us over the top." Even more than the financial support, however, was the vote of confidence that came with it. "The fact that we were building a brewery rather than closing one— their whole family thought that was the neatest thing.

Their friends did, too. It gave us the confidence that we could launch a brewery."

Despite this description of events, the care and consideration with which they had already started the process—from homebrewing to brewery visits to business and financial planning—suggests something different. Starting a brewery almost certainly seemed like a strange proposal in 1984. But Kurt and Rob had been building up to the decision for years, and while the *idea* may have been far-fetched, the proposal clearly wasn't. They'd considered everything they could think of. The proof is in the response they got to their appeal. Everybody knew they were serious, and they were willing to give them the money to give it a shot. Kurt and Rob fell short of their goal but managed to raise $63,000—easily enough to move forward with their plans.

PIONEERING MEN

There's one more important element to this story—one that echoes back through generations. It relates to the question of why. Why did Rob and Kurt decide to start a brewery? Everything up to the moment they made that decision suggested it was, at best, a long-shot proposition. Many people would look at the obstacles and conclude it was just too risky to start a brewery—that the job would require a kind of herculean effort of hard work and will that just didn't make sense. This is why most of us do not start our own breweries. And, when I asked them—multiple times—why they ultimately pulled the trigger on the project, they didn't have very persuasive answers.

Somehow, to them, the data they had gathered led them to believe it wasn't such a long shot. ("Why *wouldn't* we do this?") To understand their logic, we have to look further in the past, to the generation that immigrated to the United States. They were special people, full of temerity and daring.

Their father's side, the Widmers, came from a long line of dairy farmers. Kurt and Rob's grandfather Fredrick arrived in Scappoose, Oregon, sometime around the turn of the century with his brothers from the highlands around Bern, Switzerland. The family history about how they landed in Oregon is a little sketchy ("Someone came ahead—a neighbor?"), but there was a substantial Swiss community here. "They were invariably dairy farmers," Kurt recalls. To this day there are still Widmer dairy farmers in Tillamook.

Their mother Ann's father was named Hochscheid, and he and two brothers arrived just after the turn of the century. They hailed from Düsseldorf—a detail that would play a significant role in the brewery's story—and their grandfather has the kind of biography that might have led to a career in academia had he come from a wealthier family. He taught himself Latin and how to play the piano, and was accomplished enough to later give lessons. Still, his was a modest life, as is almost always the case with the immigrant generation.

How Grandpa Met Grandma

"The classic family story is this: There was a beauty contest at the Montavilla Theater. There used to be a theater and kind of a community center, and there used to be a beauty contest—and he was a judge. Don't ask me for more details than that, but my grandmother—his future wife—was the winner. And then not too long after she was the winner, she became Mrs. Hochscheid." As told by Kurt Widmer, with laughter supplied by Rob.

Leaving Europe in the nineteenth century meant severing one's relationship to family, to anything familiar. It meant gambling on the idea that moving to a new country, where you had no connections and probably didn't even speak the language, would somehow work out. It is the ultimate risky bet. Another immigrant in the family was that renowned homebrewer, Great-Grandma Engele (their mother's grandmother), and her story illustrates this perfectly.

Her father's brother had immigrated to North Dakota from Berlin. He knew times were tough in Berlin and telegrammed his brother back home and said he needed help on the farm—"send the boy."

Kurt picks up the story from there: "Our great-grandmother had an older brother. They book the passage and he's ready to go and at the last minute he says, 'I'm not going.' You can't blame a little kid, though. So our great-grandmother, and this is totally in keeping with her, she says, 'I'll go.' They didn't consult the uncle in North Dakota; they just *sent* her. So she gets off the train in Fargo, and the uncle thinks he's meeting 'the boy' and here's 'the girl.' It was the classic story from that time, she's like, 'I can do anything he can do but I can do it better.' So she proceeded to demonstrate that she could work as hard at whatever task that he needed done as 'the boy.'"

The population of the colonies in America made it effectively a European nation (Native American civilizations had limited influence on the culture of the colonists). And yet, they weren't the same kinds of Europeans who remained in Europe—immigrants to America were the ones who left their country behind. The traditionalists, those who supported old ways of doing things, were the ones who stayed. The members of the families who left looked for adventures, new ways, and new cultures. They were the gamblers and the risk-takers. Many of their descendants carried the nesting genes—they built up the cities of Boston and Philadelphia—but some of them had that wandering streak. They were the ones who left *again*.

It is hard to get to the West Coast, and no one arrives here by accident. It's even farther from Europe. The character of the West Coast is flavored by this propensity, and the people who live here are the kind who seek new places, who favor reinvention over tradition. They are entrepreneurial by nature. There's a reason craft brewing started and flourished most robustly on the West Coast. People like Rob and Kurt were grandchildren and great-grandchildren of people like Emma and Fredrick. They saw possibilities others overlooked, and they were willing to work to make them become reality. Some of them boarded ships and traveled across oceans; others left companies with benefits and regular paychecks and raised money to start businesses making a product no one was clamoring for.

Why did Kurt and Rob decide to build a brewery? What else would you expect from Emma Engele's great-grandsons?

DÜSSELDORF OF THE WILLAMETTE

T HE ORIGINAL WIDMER BREWERY WAS LOCATED AT 1405 Northwest Lovejoy in what is now the Pearl District. (1405 was also the address of the house they grew up in; "Our mom said it was a good omen," Rob remembers.) At the time, this previously unnamed neighborhood was a dead zone between Old Town and the freeway, a welter of nondescript two- to four-story warehouses stretching from Burnside north to the Willamette River. This neighborhood was a target for the first craft breweries because the buildings were spacious, leases were cheap, and roads were free of heavy traffic. Three of the first four craft breweries landed there—and of course, the neighborhood was anchored by the orange-brick giant that loomed from its perch on Burnside, the old Blitz-Weinhard brewery. Auspiciously, even before Rob and Kurt opened their doors, the streets smelled of malt and hops.

That first Lovejoy brewery was not, by any account, a gorgeous one. The space, which looked big enough when the building was empty, filled up quickly. Most of the equipment hadn't been made for brewing beer, and certainly none of it had been made to look beautiful, to be gazed on from a dining room through glass. Recall that, at the time, there were no small-brewery manufacturers in the country, no secondhand brewhouses to buy from growing companies. Kurt and Rob assembled their first brewery by picking up bits and pieces where they could find them—used dairy equipment (a favorite of early breweries because they were food-grade stainless steel), parts salvaged from the Olympia brewery, even tanks from a nuclear facility. A friend built a steel frame for the mash tun that "would have supported the Queen Mary if we'd wanted it to," Kurt quipped.

The brewery had a decidedly provisional quality to it. "Yeah, it was cobbled together," Kurt said. "The lids from our mash tun opened up from the side and had to be several hundred pounds—with a razor edge. Our dad rigged up some kind of chain to the ceiling and we'd raise that up and hook that."

Rob added, "It was classic stuff. We had the elevated mash tun and it was so elevated that it hit the ceiling joists, so you couldn't really stand up completely when you were on this platform stirring. The very first mash we had an oar, a paddle. It didn't work, so we grabbed pieces of pipe and we were like, 'How do we stir this?'"

By good fortune, they had a friend, Jay Rymeski, who did video production, and archival footage of the

Kurt and Rob getting ready to hand-deliver kegs in the garage of the Lovejoy brewery.

operation still exists. There you can see much younger versions of the brothers amid what is clearly secondhand equipment. The sides of vessels have roughly welded seams and the dings and patina of age. Hand-me-down kegs from the region's larger breweries are stippled with dents. The pièce de résistance is the keg-filler, pieced together from salvaged steel and an old pallet jack. The footage is all in black and white, but you have the sense that things really were monochrome—different shades of steel, iron, and damp concrete.

But the other thing you see in the video are men— the brothers are joined by their father, Ray, and several early employees—each familiar with the brewery's quirks, hopping around the brewery as it hums with life. There's both a kinetic quality, as kegs bounce around from stacks to hand trucks, and a technical one, as Kurt or Rob inspect the beer's clarity or its attenuation. It may not have been a beauty, that first brewery, but it became, after years of tinkering, a workhorse.

BUILT TO BREW ALTBIER

The brewery Kurt and Rob built was intended to make altbier. This may seem strange, not least because altbier was then and remains a very obscure style of beer. Even stranger is the idea that a brewery would make just a single type of beer. No modern brewery would launch based on such an idea—and in fact, breweries now regularly make dozens of different brands each year. This mindset is instructive, though. Until the craft beer era, breweries did just make one kind of beer. Stroh's made

Stroh's; Hamm's made Hamm's. A brewery might make a light beer variant, but the brewery name and the beer were synonymous.

The early craft brewing pioneers adopted this mindset and conceived of themselves as makers of a particular type of beer. In his recent memoir, Boston Beer founder Jim Koch describes the moment his father, a fourth-generation brewer, rummaged through boxes in the attic to find a family recipe from the nineteenth century. "If you're going to do this crazy thing," Koch recalls his father telling him, "you might as well start with the best recipe." Koch built a business plan to sell Boston Lager, a beer interchangeable with the brewery's name, Samuel Adams.

Other breweries were doing the same thing. Redhook made an ESB (strong English bitter); Sierra Nevada, a pale ale. Full Sail chose amber ale; Pete Slosberg (Pete's Wicked) put his chips on brown ale. One by one, across the country, start-ups were trying to figure out which flavor would appeal to drinkers who only understood "beer" to mean "fizzy yellow lager." There was a clear logic to this single-beer approach. The pioneering breweries had to coax these drinkers to try a beer that was unfamiliar while simultaneously educating them about the new flavors and aromas they were encountering.

Deschutes Brewery's Gary Fish, who built an empire on porter, a lightly sweet dark ale, described the laborious process he had to go through with each customer who walked into his new Bend brewpub. "Anytime someone comes and says, 'Give me the lightest thing you've got,' you immediately give them a taste of Black Butte Porter.

Once they get past the color—'I don't like dark beer'—
you say, 'Just try a sample—it's free. I'll get you the beer
that you want, but taste this first.' We figured about 80
percent of them were going, 'Oh, that's really good, I'll
have one of those.' That's how the brand grew." Every one
of the early brewers describes this same slow process—
part sales, part teacher's assistant.

Like Jim Koch, the Widmers mined their family
history to locate a beer style that might appeal to customers of the day. They found it in their grandmother's
hometown of Düsseldorf. Altbier, or "old beer," is a type
of ale that has been made by area breweries for at least
150 years. Americans associate Germany with lagers, but
until the end of the nineteenth century, the only beers
made in the northern part of Germany were ales. Ales are
easier to brew and provide a bigger contrast to lagers—a
distinction early craft brewers were keen to draw—but
Rob and Kurt didn't want to brew the ales that became
a staple in most brewpubs. "Our ancestry was German,"
Kurt explained. "When we started out, we didn't want
to do English ales." The family lineage connected them to
Düsseldorf, which had a famous local ale—"and that
was perfect."

Altbier is an interesting style of beer. It's technically an
ale; in German the word is obergärige, or "top-fermenting."
But they're also called lagerbier. After being made with
an ale-type yeast strain, they are left to ripen at cold
temperatures like a lager. This points to the twin qualities that define altbier: it's a bit fruitier than a lager, but
crisper and sharper than most ales. And here's the really

The original brewery on NW Lovejoy.

important fact: they descended from a type known as "bitterbier," characterized by stiff hopping. This is quite rare in Germany, but distinguishes altbier not just from its close, paler cousin, kölsch, but most other German beers, ales, and lagers, as well.

By chance, Kurt and Rob had a relative in Düsseldorf who worked for Schlüssel, one of the city's historic altbier-makers. Through that connection, Kurt found his way to Josef Schnitzler at Zum Uerige, the most traditional and authentic of Düsseldorf's altbier houses. Kurt booked a flight to tour the brewery and learn about the style of beer, ultimately spending a week there. Uerige is a fascinating artifact of an earlier time, almost unique in its adherence to equipment that most breweries abandoned after the world wars. After the boiling wort leaves the kettle, it travels to a large, open-topped, pan-shaped vessel to cool, and then is dribbled over a contraption of pipes running with cold water. At both stages, the wort is exposed to possible airborne contaminants. Nevertheless, the beer always turns out fresh, and free of the effect of those wild microorganisms.

Kurt was impressed by this, and realized the yeast the brewery used must have been incredibly vigorous to out-compete the wild yeast and bacteria the beer was exposed to. "Josef said, 'I'm aware of the possibility of contaminants, but my yeast can handle any and all comers,'" Kurt recounted Schnitzler telling him. The two got along famously, and Schnitzler offered to let the Widmers use that voracious yeast. This would turn out to be the most fateful moment in the visit; although altbier never became a big seller for Widmer Brothers, that yeast became the foundation for the beer that would make them famous.

After he left Düsseldorf, Kurt traveled to a small town outside Munich to visit Weihenstephan, the famous brewing academy. There he met with a professor and scientist to discuss his plans. This was where Uerige banked their yeast, and while he was there, Kurt also received another strain from Weihenstephan's collection. Nevertheless, when the Widmers later tried out the two strains on their beer, they much preferred the Uerige strain. They use it to this day.

In thinking of a signature beer, the Widmers felt altbier had a lot to offer. As a dark beer, it presented an instant visual contrast. Alts are beautiful ales; from a distance they seem opaque in their darkness, but up close the brown borders on crimson, giving them rich depth in the glass. Further contrasts: altbiers are hoppy, with an assertive bitter bite; they're ales, but German—both familiar and different. Brewers of the 1980s could make a convincing argument for any of the world's beers as potential flagships, and the Widmers guessed correctly that they'd have altbier all to themselves. They thought it would be different enough to stand out, but familiar enough to gain acceptance.

BUILDING A BREWERY FROM DAIRY TANKS AND BALING WIRE

Beer has been brewed for thousands of years. It's not terribly hard to soak malted barley in warm water and ferment the barley tea that results. What is more difficult is controlling the process to make beer precisely like the brewer intends and—the really tricky part—do it batch after batch. The way a brewery is designed will give a brewer more or less control over the process. Trying to make a sophisticated instrument out of a repurposed dairy tank was impossible, and most of the early craft brewers worked with primitive systems.

By the time they started assembling their brewery, Kurt had done quite a bit of research. "There was no internet, so I went to the library and looked at all three books that were available on brewing," he said. "It was all biochemistry that was more sophisticated than I was capable of digesting—or needing. It was also geared for really large breweries." He'd learned the process at

Ray, Rob, and Kurt prepare for the grand opening party of the original brewery on NW Lovejoy Street.

Uerige, spent years honing homebrewing techniques, and had studied the brewhouses of those few craft breweries that had already launched. Even though they were assembling the system from random parts, they wanted it to be as sophisticated as possible—and it was, after a fashion.

When you listen to the brothers describe the brewhouse, though, you might have your doubts. The mash tun *sounds* a bit crude. "We had the concepts down," Kurt said, tentatively. "It was a relatively flat dairy tank with a single outlet and it sloped a little bit toward the outlet and we had a friend build a frame out of stainless steel."

Rob continued, "It was ridiculous because the dairy tank, the walls were all bowed. There was nothing plumb, and we had all these plumb plates. So when we added the water, the grain just immediately went outside the plates."

The greatest asset a brewer had in the 1980s was ingenuity, and the Widmers put theirs to use solving the problem. They devised a system with an improvised gasket—a rubber hose clipped around the edge of the plates that would fill in the gaps where they didn't meet the walls. At first the hose floated, so they filled it with water. "It worked!" Kurt said.

"It worked," Rob agreed, "but sometimes you'd be stirring and you'd catch a clip and release the gasket."

The mash tun had a heavy lid, it was too close to the rafters, and cleaning it was a monumental chore. Yet despite all this, in terms of function, it was sophisticated. Their system was capable of a technique called step-mashing, which takes fuller advantage of the enzymes in barley. This was the technique Uerige used, and it's standard all across Germany. Step-mashing requires being able to heat the water in the mash tun during the process to different precise temperatures, or "steps." Most breweries just did infusion mashing—pouring in water at a single temperature and letting it sit. With step-mashing, the Widmers could control body thickness and the fermentability of their beer, and it allowed them more consistency from batch to batch.

As they worked with the mash tun, they muscled it into shape. "We learned to pump water into the bottom, under the plate, so it floated the bed at the same time that we were stirring in," Kurt said, describing the process of making a tea with malted barley, the first stage in brewing. "We realized that in the interest of efficiency, if we could do two batches a day … I mean, everything starts out clean and you don't really get it dirty in the first batch. We learned as we went. The first two thousand batches we changed something large or small every time."

The mash tun serves as a good symbol for the entire brewery at that stage—it was capable of making high-quality beer that was ahead of its time, but required an enormous amount of effort to do so. Time and again, this theme repeated itself.

The Brewing Process

Breweries are fairly simple operations. There are many variations, but the basics are always the same. Beer starts when malted barley or other grains are infused with warm water. This releases enzymes that convert the grain starches into sugars and washes them from the grain—something like the way coffee or tea is made. That process happens in a vessel called the mash tun. Next, the liquid, called wort, is separated from the grain and sent to the kettle, where it will be boiled with hops. Depending on when the hops are added, they may contribute bitterness, flavor, or aroma to the beer. This series of steps is conducted in the brewhouse, or what brewers sometimes call the "hot side."

Once the wort is boiled, it is chilled and sent to a special tank for fermentation. Brewers add yeast at this point, which consume the sugars in the wort, turning them to alcohol. Fermentation takes a few days in ales, and up to two weeks for lagers. Finally, the beer is sent to a conditioning tank to clarify or, in the case of lagers, ripen. In some cases, brewers may add hops at this stage to infuse the beer with aromatics. Brewers sometimes call this part of the brewery the "cold side."

A few key words to remember:

- **Mash**: The slurry of malted barley and water.
- **Lauter**: The process of separating liquid from grain.
- **Wort:** The sugary liquid that is produced during the brewing process, but before fermentation has turned it into beer.
- **Kettle**: The vessel in which the wort is boiled; this is when hops are added.
- **Fermenters and conditioning tanks**: Where fermentation and aging happen.
- **Pitching yeast**: When brewers add yeast to chilled wort, it's known as "pitching."
- **Dry hopping**: The process of steeping hops in finished beer to infuse it with aromas.
- **Ale**: A beer fermented at warmer temperatures (usually 60–72 degrees), producing fruity or spicy flavor compounds. These beers are ready to serve shortly after fermentation.
- **Lager**: A beer fermented at cooler temperatures (usually 45–55 degrees), which inhibits flavor-producing compounds. Lager yeasts typically produce rough off-flavors during fermentation and the beer needs to be aged—"lagered"—to rid the beer of them.

Another piece of equipment that required an enormous amount of energy was the filter. One of the final steps in brewing is clarifying beer so it is perfectly clear in the glass. Many modern breweries skip this step, and craft beer fans often like to see a bit of haze; to our modern eye, it suggests a handcrafted product. But in 1984, Kurt and Rob wanted customers to know that their beer was as refined as anything on the market. This wasn't just the moonshine equivalent of beer—it was a quality product.

Filters were expensive, though, so they found one that fit the budget. Like the mash tun, it got the job done, but in the most laborious way possible. When they recalled working with that filter, the brothers almost seemed to sag from fatigue. "It would be one of those deals," Rob explained of a routine event, "where with a ten-barrel batch you'd get so you've got two kegs left and the filter would clog. So you've got to tear it down and clean it up. But every keg was precious and time was not, so."

The filter was such a trial that even BridgePort's founding brewer, Karl Ockert, recalled it. "I remember going over there one night and they were filtering, and it was *late*. And you could see sections of beer moving through the pipe and then it would clog up the filter and they would have to break it all down. They were just hating life with this thing."

Again, there is the flavor of metaphor in this piece of equipment. On the one hand, it wasn't strictly necessary. The beer was dark, and people might not have noticed a bit of haze—or cared. But like so much else, Rob and Kurt didn't know what to expect, and given the choice between a quickly kegged, slightly hazy beer and a clarion beer that took hours to filter, they took the slow, hard road.

Stories of this type are legion, but some of the clever work-arounds saved time and still bring a smile to the men remembering them. One of the best dates to one of their first batches of beer, which was brewed on a cold winter day. When it came time to add the yeast, they encountered a problem. "We really had no heat for the warehouse for our brewery," Kurt said. "The fermenters were not insulated, and the ambient temperature was so low. We went in and pitched and the wort started to cool." Yeast is a living organism, and if wort gets too cold, it goes dormant. Rob smiled as he recalled what came next. "That's kind of a famous story of Kurt and Ann running home and getting the electric blankets off their bed to wrap around the tanks to get them warm enough to ferment." It worked; the wort warmed up, the yeast roused themselves, and soon the beer was fermenting away.

THE OTHER FOUNDING WIDMER: RAY

Like these, many—if not most—of the early stories Rob and Kurt tell are ones of clever jury-rigging equipment, not actual brewing. And this brings us to one of the most important members of the Widmer team during these early years: the master jury-rigger, father Ray Widmer.

Ray was such an important figure in the early days of the brewery that when we sat down for our first interview, Kurt started speaking before I'd even asked a question. "I don't know how far back you want to go," he said. "But I think it's important from my perspective that our dad was critical—even before we started. The reason I bring that up is that growing up we had this model of a man who worked very, very hard, seven days a week, rarely took vacation, went to work sick as a dog. He was our model." Throughout the multiple discussions we had, Kurt and Rob would constantly mention their father's early influence, either directly, as the inventor of some improvised toggle or widget, or indirectly, on the way they conducted their work.

His biggest contribution in the early years was his ingenuity, without which it's difficult to see how the brothers could have succeeded. Ray Widmer had grown up on a dairy farm where troubleshooting was a daily necessity, and he carried that through his life. When Rob and Kurt pieced together their brewery, they were constantly confronting challenges to make it work better—or at all. Ray's handiwork was everywhere.

"Our dad was remarkable," Kurt said, a few minutes into our first interview.

"Yeah, he'd do stuff without spending *any* money," Rob said. "Good farm boy, you know, working with what he had."

"Depression-era farm boy. We would say, 'This is what we want it to do,' and he'd say, 'Okay, I get it.' And he'd make it work—that's what he'd done all his life."

Kurt elaborated, describing one of Ray's early innovations. "I don't know how long it would have taken to figure out that grain hopper. At that point Great Western would sell one ton of malt in a cardboard box, and our little red truck could haul one ton. So we would go over there and say, 'Dad, how are we going to get it out of

Rob, Ray, and Kurt Widmer.

that truck?' And he'd say, 'Well, we need an auger.' So he went and got an auger and hooked it up—suspended it from the ceiling on a chain—so when we came in we could put that into the box. It worked great. And then we thought, 'How are we going to get this out?' And he riveted two channels of steel and made a slide-gate. It would have taken me a long time to figure that one out. And it worked perfect. There were countless things, and we'd say this is what we need this to do, and he'd say, 'Okay, I think I can do that.' It always just worked; it was always bulletproof."

Angel Marquez was one of the Widmers' first employees, and he regularly worked with Ray. "I don't think they could have made it without him," he told me. "Not without a) his moral support, and b) his expertise. He was a much more experienced man in those days. They weren't naïve men; they just didn't have the experience they needed to get that brewery off to a success. I mean, they didn't buy a brewery, they built one."

Ray's most famous design, the keg-filler, was captured in photos, early video footage, and the memory of the people who used it—like Sebastian Pastore, who came to the brewery in the 1980s after graduating from Reed and stayed for decades. When he began describing the contraption, it was with a blend of amazement and amusement. It was entirely self-designed, pieced together from different parts and machines. It was completely provisional, but also perfectly functional. The Widmers resisted bottling their beer for a dozen years, so every drop of beer they brewed went into kegs—it was a critical piece of equipment. Everyone seems to agree that the keg-filler was Ray's masterpiece.

Ray's Keg-Filler

SEBASTIAN PASTORE: "You wouldn't believe it; the racking apparatus was an old pallet jack with these two forks that you put these round Golden Gate kegs in with the bung facing up. Then you'd put the keg on there, and then Ray would take the apparatus. It was two old pieces of Unistrut [steel pieces] that had been bolted together that held a nylon hose coming through this old rubber bung and going down into the keg. And then there was a little bent-up copper tube with a ball valve on it where the gas came out."

Rob, Kurt, and Ray with some of the original "nuclear power plant" equipment in the Lovejoy brewery.

ROB WIDMER: "Our keg counterfiller, it was awesome. He used this pallet jack that we had, that was the cradle, and this thing—it was just a hose and tube and stuff that you had to hold. But they were lively, though, belly-bung Golden Gate kegs. He would fill it and lift it off and you'd have just a couple seconds to drive the bung in. And sometimes, if you didn't hit it squarely, it would be like holding your finger over a garden hose. And frequently—it was kind of random which way it would aim—but if it was my dad, you know, he could take a bath. Seeing my dad soaked head to toe with beer will stay with me all my life."

There is a more subtle and pervasive influence Ray had on the brewery: in the way his sons carried their father with them, even long after he had passed. Their reverence for him is clear in the way Kurt and Rob speak about Ray, but even more than that, much of what composes their personalities, ethics, and habits seems to have come directly from him. Listening to people talk about the men is an uncanny experience because the descriptions are often interchangeable.

Ray was, first and foremost, a hard worker. By the time Rob and Kurt started their brewery, he'd already retired. Yet even at retirement age, he threw himself into his work like his sons. His help was indispensable, and he continued to work even after they started brewing. Kurt and Rob joked at one point that if they'd ever worked an employee as hard as they worked their dad, he'd never have come back the next day. "We're working physically very hard and we're in our late twenties, early thirties, and he's mid-sixties," Kurt said, almost apologetically. (Kurt, himself a man in his mid-sixties when he spoke those words, seemed to have a new sense of what they had asked Ray to do.) "There were days that he would leave and he would look ashen gray."

If they'd been speaking about anyone but their father, these kinds of anecdotes might have sounded almost sadistic. "I was thinking our sisters aren't going to be too forgiving if we kill our dad," Kurt joked. "But you know, good ol' farm boy, he was up at five every morning and he never missed a day." But he was their father, and even at that late date, with his adult sons launching their own business, he was still acting as a role model. They joke

The original Widmer crew: Rob, Kurt, and their father, Ray, tasting Altbier.

about it now because they admired him so much. The jokes are a way of honoring these final lessons.

Another quality that describes all three—and one that was not quite so universally celebrated—was their proclivity to save a buck. Pastore didn't just call Ray a MacGyver—he called him a thrifty MacGyver. "Ray was a Depression baby," he continued. "He was a genuinely nice guy, but he had some really strong qualities, and the strongest quality Ray exemplified was thrift. Ray was the thriftiest guy you have ever met."

Marquez agreed. "He was very frugal. He didn't wear nice clothes, he didn't drive a nice car. He did eventually get a new Subaru, but it was a base-model car. He was never flashy."

That made him a perfect fit for a brewery where cash was in short supply, but that thriftiness carried on long after the coffers started rattling with coins. Pastore, who became one of the most trusted members of the leadership as the brewery grew, constantly had to justify expenditures.

"That whole value system, and that whole process of building the original brewery, never left them," Pastore said. "Kurt was continually coming and trying to get me to, you know, find a deal. 'Oh! I can't believe we're going to pay Mueller $50,000 for a hot water tank. We can find a used one and put it in there.'" Eventually, Kurt and Rob would always spend money to improve the brewery, but their first instinct, like that of their father, was to see if there was a cheaper way to do things.

There were other pieces, too. Rob and Kurt are famously quiet men. So was Ray. This sometimes disadvantaged them—at Dogfish Head and Boston Beer, charismatic owners became the media-friendly faces of the company. But the sons of Ray Widmer were never going to be big personalities you saw on television. On the other hand, they *were* the kind of guys you might see pouring samples at the grocery store (as I did not too long ago in a local Fred Meyer). They continued to interact with the public, person by person, the whole time they worked for the brewery. There was something old-fashioned about this grassroots approach, something like what you'd expect from a Depression-era farm boy who eventually became a farm-machinery salesman.

For those who worked alongside Ray, he became a beloved figure in the brewhouse. Marquez was still in

The Widmer delivery truck parked in front of the Lovejoy brewery.

high school when he first arrived at the brewery. (He was actually 15, and when Kurt and Rob discovered he couldn't legally work there, they had to tell him to come back when he was 16.) He's worked for Widmer Brothers ever since. "I miss Ray tremendously. When Ray left us I was very, very sad. It felt like I lost a family member." The brewery came to be known as Widmer Brothers, but it might as easily have been called Widmer and Sons.

BREWING BEER (FINALLY)

Rob and Kurt signed the lease on their first brewery in late 1984 and, with Ray's help, began assembling their equipment. They brewed their first batch of Altbier on January 26, 1985—the period of electric blanket fermenter-cozies. It was a promising batch, and Kurt even admitted it was "way better than any homebrew I ever

Rob delivering kegs to Oregon Brewers Festival.

made." Nevertheless, once it had fermented out, they tasted it and summarily dumped all ten barrels down the drain.

This isn't too surprising. The first batch of any new recipe may not turn out precisely as the brewer intended. It's even more common when you add new brewery equipment to the equation—and perhaps inevitable on the maiden voyage of a pieced-together Frankenbrewery like the Widmers had. What *is* surprising—and revealing—is that they then went on to dump the next nine batches of Altbier, too. "It just wasn't right," they both agreed.

Even now, forty years into craft brewing, a story like this would be surprising. If the flavor hasn't been perfectly dialed in, modern brewers reason, it's acceptable to sell a beer that tastes fine on its own merits and is free of faults or off flavors. Brewers can always continue to refine their recipes—and many do, often years after launch. But now imagine the mid-1980s. Only the very rare world traveler would even have heard of the altbier style, and nobody would have known what it was supposed to taste like. Those ten batches of beer amounted to 400 kegs, 3,100 gallons, and nearly 25,000 pints of beer. The Widmers spent thousands of dollars on ingredients, hundreds more in salary and operations costs, and were earning nothing on these perfectly drinkable batches of beer. It didn't occur to either of them to release Altbier before it was exactly what they wanted it to be, so batch after batch went down the drain. "We made constant improvements. The good news was that during all of this time we were brewing clean beer," Rob said of those batches.

This anecdote hints at things more pervasive. It's actually not even an anecdote—Rob and Kurt just mentioned it in passing. It's not a fact very many people have heard, and it isn't featured in the official biographies, perhaps in part because it involves an obscure beer in the brewery's past. That they dumped this beer is instructive, however, because it's just one of the many examples of how committed to quality Kurt and Rob have been throughout their brewing lives. And even that is not something the brewery explicitly celebrates—though it's a fundamental part of the Widmer DNA.

As soon as they could, for example, they hired a microbiologist to set up a lab. This is uncommon today and was much rarer in the 1980s. Once they started bottling,

Widmer began an in-house sensory evaluation program to assess the beer leaving the brewery. They also set up a "library" of released beers, which allowed them to assess beers as they aged and also gave them a standard reference to compare with beer that went out into the market. Examples like this litter their story.

Eventually, of course, they did brew a batch they were proud enough to release to the world, and in late winter of 1985 they sold their first keg to the Louis the XIV on Sandy Boulevard, one of those old Portland taverns that is lost to us now. Local media had gotten wind of this new-brewery storm that was taking over the city (two already in production, more in planning), and even before the Widmers could get to market, *The Oregonian* and local news had been reporting on their progress. To their surprise, they had taverns like the Louis the XIV contacting them to buy kegs before they had beer. After years of planning, months of building out the brewery, and weeks of test-brewing, Widmer Brewing was finally ready to launch. The City of Roses was about to learn about their new favorite beer style, a nineteenth-century dark ale from Düsseldorf. The wind-up had been costly and exhausting, but now everything was looking great.

A DRAFT CITY

THE CITY OF PORTLAND, OREGON, OCCUPIES A special place in the beer world. Situated forty miles north of the hop fields of the Willamette Valley and about a mile south of one of two major American malt-houses, it has been the center of one of America's most active brewing regions. As recently as the 1980s, several regional breweries from Seattle to Portland managed to survive the era of consolidation, and, for a century and a half, downtown was home to the Weinhard brewery. But more than even this rich history, the craft era has distinguished the city.

About 85 percent of the beer sold nationally is tradi-tional mass-market lager, either domestic or imported. Craft beer is increasingly hard to define, but if we call it everything that's not mass-market lager, craft accounts for the remaining 15 percent of the market. In Oregon, craft's share is 30 percent, and Portland is approaching 50 percent craft. Even more remarkably, it's now a lot harder to find a mass-market lager on draft than it is to find an IPA; more than four-fifths of the city's taps pour craft beer. Of the craft beer sold in the state, the large majority is brewed in Oregon. This market penetration not only far exceeds any city in the United States, but is now ahead of places like London and Brussels.

Which raises the obvious question: how did we get here?

A RIVER CITY

Portland is often compared to its sister cities along the West Coast—Vancouver, British Columbia; Seattle; and San Francisco—but there are many ways in which it is unusual among this group. It's a port city—the Columbia River provides deepwater access—but it's not coastal. Rather, Portland is a river city, like the Rust Belt towns of the Midwest. Carl Abbott, a professor at Portland State University who has written extensively about the city and was the moving force behind establishing the university's vaunted urban studies department, described the Rose City beautifully in his 1983 book, *Portland*:

> *River cities are usually working cities, and Portland is a city built around a working river. A lake port like Chicago can beautify its waterfront with beaches and boulevards and hide freighters and barges behind its back alleys.... Portland's front door still opens on to the lower twenty miles of the Willamette River that gave it birth. Its open acknowledgement of the world of hard work and heavy loads separates Portland from other western cities just as surely as its misty climate and dark green hills. Its*

first cousins are not glamour cities such as San Francisco or Denver. They are other solid and sober river cities of middle America, from Pittsburgh to St. Louis.

Abbott observed that coastal cities look outward, to the distant lands connected by shipping, while river cities look inward. When I spoke to him for this project, Abbott reemphasized this point. "Seattle looks to the world, Portland looks to the Columbia Basin. We have a much more extensive hinterland inland than Seattle does, but Seattle's got the global connections." Cosmetically, they have a lot in common; neighborhoods in the cities could easily stand in for each other. Both are known for their great restaurants, outdoor lifestyles, farmers markets, and snowcapped volcano views.

But the cultures differ in notable ways. Shortly after I began writing about beer in the 1990s, a Washington brewer told me something fascinating. "We love Oregon beer!" he said, before going on to list the breweries that had found favor in Seattle. "But we can't give our beer away in Portland." Seattleites, with their urbane embrace of the world, welcome beer from all over. It was the first time I'd heard that complaint from a Washington brewer, but hardly the last. Over the next twenty years I heard it every time I asked why I couldn't find a Washington brewery's beer here. Portlanders, looking inward, exalt local breweries but spurn outsiders.

Stuart Ramsay is an expat Scotsman who began working for breweries in Washington and Portland in the 1980s. Both cities embrace local in a way they wouldn't on the East Coast, he said. "It goes back to this great thing about the Pacific Northwest, which is the fact that if you're making something, people will at least darken your door to try it." The big difference, though, is "an element of provincialism in Oregon and in Portland that made beer successful, because you support your businesses—to a fault." To this day, Oregon has more breweries, a greater embrace of local beer, and more big breweries than Washington—and Portland more than Seattle.

Of course, there are many provincial river cities in the country, so that alone hardly accounts for Portland's unique beer culture. Every city has its own unique stew of circumstances, but in Portland's case, public policy played a large role, as odd as that sounds. A big part of the Rose City's renaissance as a brewing capital was built on the infrastructure available throughout its intact neighborhoods. Unlike so many American cities, Portland was never hollowed out by suburbanization in the 1960s and '70s. And this is a legacy of an unusual cadre of immigrants in the 1960s.

Portland would become famous for its quirky, Portlandia personality, but in the 1960s, it had a different reputation. Leave it to Abbott, whose field is urban studies, to notice this. People in that earlier generation, Abbott said, "were coming in because Portland was earning a reputation as this wonky, neighborhood-oriented place doing good planning. I would call it a policy-wonk generation rather than a techie generation."

Those policy wonks used Portland as a laboratory for preserving the urban core. "Starting at the end of the

1960s and going into the '70s there was a strong neighborhood conservation movement," Abbott said. "A lot of that was around land use planning, conserving the old housing stock." Portland did suburbanize, but only modestly, preserving the commercial centers that continued to anchor neighborhoods across the city. What effect did this have on the character of the town? "I was particularly impressed back in 1980 or so of all the neighborhood movie theaters that were still functioning. In most cities there were no neighborhood theaters left. There was downtown stuff for the artsy people, then there were the cineplexes."

You know what else flourished next to those theaters? Neighborhood pubs and taverns. Oregon has long had an unusually healthy pub trade—something the United States as a whole lost following Prohibition and the introduction of canned beer in 1935. Most Americans drink beer at home, and currently just one in ten beers is consumed at a pub. But back in 1984, when the Widmers were getting started, nearly a quarter of the beer in Oregon was sold on draft. That figure was probably higher in Portland, where grabbing a pint has always been a local habit. That was an invaluable audience for small breweries that had to sell beer on draft (bottling lines are expensive).

One of the best examples of Portland's connection to taverns was its forty-eighth mayor, Bud Clark, who was elected in 1984, the same year the Widmers started their brewery. Clark was an unknown when he started running, but voters responded to his populist message. His appeal resonated in large part because he was a saloon owner who depended on volunteers from his Goose Hollow Inn tavern—and who won by appealing to the kinds of people who went to pubs.

"All my volunteers came out of the tavern," he told me. "They were going door-to-door." More than that, volunteers developed a grassroots appeal that spread throughout the taverns. It started with a campaign button that read, "Bud Clark is serious." It was a pre-internet bid at virality, where the button would cause people to start conversations. "We had these pickle jars that we get a lot of here at the Goose Hollow," Clark explained, "and we set up in taverns all over the city these jars with buttons and 'Donate to the Bud Clark for mayor campaign.' And this couple would go collect the money and put in more buttons."

He famously would peddle or paddle (in a canoe) around the city on door-to-door excursions, but "on Saturdays I'd go up to Lombard Street and go to the taverns and talk to people, because that was the working-class neighborhood, and they like to go to the taverns on the weekend." There are not many cities in which a publican would win an election for mayor, but that was a big part of Clark's appeal. He beat Frank Ivancie, a powerful incumbent, in the primary in one of the biggest upsets in city history. "A lotta things happen in taverns, you know!" Clark said, laughing.

Kurt and Rob understood the value of the local pub trade, and it was one of the main facts that led them to believe they could successfully launch a brewery here. "From memory," Kurt said, "22 percent of total beer sales were draft at that point." (He was very close—it was 23 percent.) Draft beer drinkers were considered more sophisticated, and the Widmers thought they would be willing to pay more for a premium product. "Imported cars sell well here, coffee, quality of life stuff," Kurt said.

Rob added, "There always has been an appreciation for outdoor recreation and clean water, quality of life. People were willing to pay more if something was clearly better."

This was a calculation made by all the pioneering breweries in the city. Just around the corner, Karl Ockert and Dick Ponzi were designing BridgePort as a pub-based brewery. Brian and Mike McMenamin were interested in brewing beer to serve in their still-small collection of pubs, and Art Larrance and Fred Bowman were beginning plans for the brewpub that would become Portland Brewing on Northwest Flanders—just four blocks from the Widmers. Eventually, of course, breweries would begin packaging their beer in bottles (though the Widmers held out for a dozen years, until 1996), but Portland has always remained a brewpub town. As craft brewing continued to gather steam, the large majority of breweries started out with a little pub and only later moved to bottles or cans—if they ever did. Even well into the second decade of the new century, most of the city's breweries are built with pubs to which you can go and enjoy a pint.

To Portlanders, who have always sought out local beer in pubs, this seems completely natural, but it's unusual nationally. Most cities lacked the city-planning background Abbott described. Throughout the '60s and '70s they experienced large-scale suburbanization, and neighborhood-based theaters and pubs closed up. People bought their beer at grocery or liquor stores and took it home to drink. Craft breweries in most American cities, when they began opening in the 1980s and '90s, were usually designed to make packaged beer, with a pub as an afterthought.

It's not coincidental that the number of breweries started spiking in the last five years. As recently as 2010—deep within the Great Recession—there were just 1,750 breweries in the country. The revitalization of downtowns accelerated after the Great Recession, just as small breweries, most of them sporting a tasting room, exploded. Now there are over 7,000 in the United States, many scattered throughout neighborhoods that are rebuilding their infrastructure of local restaurants, coffee shops, pubs, and drinking halls.

What Rob and Kurt saw when they looked out over the landscape was a city that drank beer in pubs and thirsted for local products. They were insular and protective of local business, but adventuresome enough to try new things. The draft business was so good in Portland that the early breweries all started selling draft-only beer. The McMenamins built an empire on pubs, and there are still very few breweries in the city that don't have a pub component to their business. This is entirely different from most other towns, where pub culture is still nowhere near as strong as Portland's, and where most breweries focus on bottles.

(And Washington's breweries still can't sell their beer here.)

DELIVERING THE BEER THEY BREWED

One of the most important elements of the Widmer Brothers story has to do with a little-understood layer in the beer business: distribution. Following Prohibition, the United States adopted a regulatory structure to limit breweries' control over the sale of beer. Rather than letting breweries sell directly to retailers—which in countries like the UK led to brewery-owned pub empires—regulators adopted a "three-tier" system, with distributors (also called wholesalers) in between retailers and breweries. In this system, breweries sell to distributors, and distributors sell to grocery stores and pubs.

Wholesalers are largely invisible; in fact, when you see them driving around town, the logos splashed across the trucks are always for the beer they distribute, not their own company. Nevertheless, they play an enormously important role. It is the distributor, not the brewery, that makes direct sales. When distributors arrive at a pub looking to place some of their kegs on tap there, they—not the brewery—decide which product to promote. Modern distributors regularly represent multiple breweries, and this gives them outsized influence on the success of certain breweries.

Each state oversees the way distribution works, and some allow breweries to participate in two of the three tiers. In 1980s Oregon, breweries were allowed to distribute their own beer. Paul Romain, who was for decades the beer and wine wholesalers' powerful lobbyist, describes the situation at the time: "Oregon always had what was called a two-tier system of distribution. You could be in the manufacturing and wholesaling end, but you couldn't have any interest in retail."

The distribution laws were fine when the beer companies were large regional or national players. But as the first craft breweries were looking to go to market, they wanted to be able to sell their own beer at their own breweries. They had no name recognition, sold a product consumers didn't yet understand, and made more expensive beer in small quantities. Selling beer in their own on-site pubs was an obvious solution, but it was against the law. If it seems inconceivable that they couldn't do so, consider this a signpost about how far we've come. The laws didn't allow for a brewpub partly because it had never occurred to anyone to set one up.

Working with Romain, the McMenamins, BridgePort, and Widmer pushed to have the law changed. Distributors were not keen to see their piece of the market diminish and opposed throwing open the door to little breweries who wanted to act as their own retailers *and* distributors. As a compromise, the little guys proposed keeping the two-tier option open, but expanding it. Romain described their proposal: "Why don't we set up a scheme where you in effect pick the tier you want to be in? If you want to be in distribution and production, fine, that's the brewery license. If you want to be in production and retail, that's the brewpub license. You pick." In fairly short order, they managed to get legislation pushed through to make their idea Oregon law.

Initially, the Widmers had planned to have a brewpub, too, but their brewery building wasn't big enough for a pub, nor did they have the money to build out space for one. Even so, they were still thinking this was a middle-term plan—Kurt, recall, was attracted to beer precisely because of his pub-going experiences in Germany. To keep that option open, they began by looking for a distributor.

Even though there were far fewer brands for sale in Portland at the time, each brewery had its own wholesaler, so there were actually more distributors. But because distributors and breweries had such a tight relationship, it made it difficult for the smaller breweries to find a distributor willing to take them on. "We wanted to use wholesalers," Rob said, "but they were like the bankers." They couldn't see the value in working with these new breweries and their tiny volumes. It looked like a lot more work for very little reward. Needless to say, no one at the time could see thirty-five years into the future, to the time when more than two-thirds of the draft trade would be made up of these "micro" breweries.

Left with little choice, the brothers decided to distribute their beer themselves. It meant giving up on the brewpub plan, and it meant having to hump their own kegs all over town, but it also meant they could personally sell their beer to retailers. They began making deliveries in a Datsun pickup truck that has since become an iconic symbol for the brewery. (In fact, of all the symbols the brewery has used over the years, that truck seems to have the most staying power.) "The Datsun was the pride of the fleet!" Rob said with affection, then added: "That *was* our fleet at the time."

As Kurt and Rob prepared to sell their first keg, a surprising thing happened: they started getting press. The idea of new breweries opening up was fascinating to Portlanders, and the papers and TV stations were covering Widmer and BridgePort as they fired up their mash tuns for the first time. For skeleton crews already overworked at the brewhouse, this was a godsend: it meant their first sales came to them. "This guy came and he had an account, doesn't exist anymore, called Louis the XIV on Sandy," Kurt recalls. "He said, 'I want to be your first account.' Rob and I were like, 'Cool! We've got our first customer!'" Almost immediately, self-distribution seemed to be working out all right.

First Account: Louis the XIV

KURT: "We'd never delivered anything before and he told us he had to work another job, but his wife will be there, she'd be expecting us. So we throw a keg in the red truck—"

ROB: "Two kegs, he bought two kegs."

KURT: "Did he? Okay, so we throw a couple kegs in the truck and get out there and we didn't have any idea what to do, and she's kind of looking at us and said, 'Oh, the kegs are down in the cooler, down in the basement.' Ah, of course. He had built this wooden slide, or chute … Anyhow, it was all Rob's fault!" They begin to laugh.

"I guess we thought that—it was pretty apparent that we couldn't just let the keg go down the chute, so Rob was going to walk beside it and coax it down. That lasted about six inches and then it just raced down. It's dark down there and we hear a crash—they're stainless, they're like bowling balls, those old Golden Gate kegs. Crash! Crash! Going through walls, just doing horrible things down there. We looked at each other, and then we looked at her, and we thought, 'We're out of business.' The first delivery and we're done here. It was like, 'Well Rob, I hope you enjoyed yourself while it lasted.'

"And without batting an eye she goes, 'Oh, that happens.' So we went down and turned on the lights and recovered the kegs, put them in the cooler, hooked 'em up, and said, 'You might want to wait just a *little* bit, a couple hours, to let things calm down,' and she goes, 'Yeah, yeah, I got it.' And so that was our first delivery."

━━━━━━━━━━━━━━━━━━━━━━━━━━━━━━━━━

The brothers were young and hungry, and they turned self-distribution to their advantage. Because they only had one client and a very stable slate of tavern accounts, distributors didn't offer much in the way of service. "Wholesalers were so bad then," Rob said. "I mean, you had to have Bud, Miller, and Coors, and so the wholesalers would tell the retailers when they were going to be there, and they said, 'Better be there with a check.'" There was no incentive to offer better service. For Kurt and Rob, the reason was clear—they cherished every tap handle they had and were willing to do anything to make sure a publican was happy. "It was so easy to out-service them. We would bend over backwards 24-7, clean up our messes. We would fix problems."

"In the early days, we told accounts that we would deliver beer within an hour if it was a call that came in Monday through Friday from eight to five," Kurt said. "We told them that we would deliver 24-7 within two hours. *And* we gave them our home phones."

Self-distribution also gave them visibility. If you called for a keg of beer from Widmer Brewing, a Widmer showed up in an old truck to deliver it. "People loved it, once they started catching on—Kurt and I were delivering the kegs," Rob said. Kurt added, "We would drive through town doing deliveries with eight kegs in the back, and people would be honking and cheering and everything. I can't tell you how many guys pulled up beside me and said, 'Where's the party?!'"

The honeymoon period petered out before long. Tavern owners who wanted something new and exciting reached out, but they were the minority. This is another one of those situations our modern minds find difficult to process: most drinkers didn't *want* something new. When Widmer Brewing debuted, national beer consumption was at an all-time high. There didn't appear to be pent-up demand for a new kind of beer. Tavern owners had a great thing going on. They had four to six taps, always with the same beer, and they had customers who always ordered the same thing. The bar business was clean and easy. It was little more than cashing checks, something Kurt recalled with amusement.

"How many guys would come in in the morning, count the receipts from the night before, take something to the bank—they go off and the bar manager comes in. Put in an hour or two a day. We saw that time and time again. 'Where's so-and-so?' 'Oh, he's out on the golf course.' 'Oh, yeah, it's ten o'clock, what am I thinking?'"

To break into this safe, fixed world, the Widmers needed to offer something more than just a weird, hoppy beer. They soon hit on the value of a buck as one incentive. "We went through a really quick, desperate learning curve there," Kurt said. "At first we'd go in and say the beer's so much better, but that had only limited appeal. But then we said you're going to make an extra hundred dollars a keg. Then it was like, 'Okay! Now we're talking!'"

"It was a quarter," Rob said. "I remember if you charge a quarter more per glass, you make up the difference right there, but you could charge fifty cents more. Some places got it, but it still wasn't a slam dunk."

Profit Margins

KURT WIDMER: "So let's say that major domestic was $50 a keg. We were coming in at $68. We had no experience with accounts. Fifty was the going rate, whether it was Bud, Miller, or Lite. We worked out an equation that we could customize for every account. This is Joe's Bar and Grill and you pay fifty bucks and you sell 200 glasses of major domestic at a dollar a glass—two hundred gross, minus fifty bucks, a hundred and fifty net. Very clear. So you'd get a keg of Widmer, 200 glasses, same size keg, sell it for two bucks a glass. They're like, 'Two bucks a glass?!' 'Trust me,' we say, 'they'll pay for it.' So then the gross is $400. Minus $68, so here's your profitability over major domestic brands."

They also began to realize that a bar really didn't need six taps of mass-market lager—not really. Kurt described what they'd say to barmen: "Do you really need Bud, Coors, Bud Light, Coors Light, and Miller Lite? Do you need all these taps devoted to major domestics? Why can't you carry Miller Lite in the bottle?" Taken together, their sales pitch was one part beer, one part profit margin, and one part handle-pilfering. This same conversation was happening in taverns across the city as BridgePort and Widmer and, in 1986, Portland Brewing began trying to finagle tap handles.

It was a good pitch, particularly when the tavern hadn't carried a craft beer before. But it only worked if people were actually buying the beer—and that was where Rob and Kurt started to encounter turbulence.

DARK, BITTER BEER IN AN AGE OF LIGHT, MILD LAGERS

The biggest challenge of this era was trying to nudge drinkers away from what they thought of as "beer" to something stronger and more unusual. The Widmers had thought carefully about the ale their brewery would produce, but it was proving to be a challenge to sell. And it didn't require a nudge to move people to altbier, which was both dark *and* bitter—it took a shove.

One early incident captures what they were up against. Shortly after they started selling beer, a nonprofit contacted them for a keg donation. They had been out on the streets already trying to get people to drink their beer, so this seemed like a great opportunity to put their beer in front of more people. Rob relayed what happened: "The afternoon of the event I got a call and they said, 'What are you guys tryin' to do? We had to go and *buy* beer.' They just came unglued. First they said it was bad, it had gone off, and I thought, 'Oh crap, what did we do?' I went out and tasted it and that was the way it was supposed to taste." The point, Rob explained, was that Altbier was so far outside people's expectations that they thought something must be wrong with it.

A big part of this was the color. Altbier isn't deeply brown, and certainly not black like a porter or stout. Nevertheless, "what we learned fairly quickly," Rob said, "was that Altbier fell into the dark beer category—and nobody wanted dark beer at all."

The other, more substantial hurdle was the bitterness. In Germany, altbiers range from mildly to assertively bitter, and Widmer pushed theirs to the limit. The brewery still proudly sells their Altbier, and if you go down to the pub and order a pint, it's immediately obvious: even by today's standards, Altbier is impressively bitter.

At one point, while they were developing the beer, they sent a sample over to some of the brewers at the Blitz-Weinhard brewery to test the bitterness level. The brewmaster called once the results came back. Kurt relayed the conversation: "He said, 'Do you guys want to take a guess?' I said, 'Thirty-five?' He said, 'Not even close.' I think it was seventy-five. Honestly, it was overhopped. It was *ridiculously* overhopped." By way of comparison, a domestic lager from the era would have had around fifteen units of bitterness.

Even when they dialed back the hopping, it was still hugely bitter by the standards of the day. Although too bitter for most palates, it remains a legendary beer in Portland lore: its assertiveness made it a favorite among those who prized its intensity, its outlandishness. Ask old-timers of a certain bent, and you'll hear them describe their first encounters with that beer; they inevitably refer to it as the best beer the Widmers ever brewed. One of those fans was local beer writer Fred Eckhardt. In his column for *The Oregonian*, he named Altbier the "Beer of the Year" for 1985, calling it "a sturdy, copper-colored delight, bathed in Oregon hops." Indeed it was.

In the first six months of business, the Widmers tried everything they could to move the drinking population beyond the diehards. Since there weren't enough Altbier fans in the wild, Kurt and Rob deployed a scheme, which they later heard Heineken had also used, called "designated drinkers." They made it *look* like there was a lot of demand. Once they'd managed to land a precious account, they'd put the plan into motion. They'd send a group of friends in for a night of drinking and try to drink through as much of the keg as possible. "Then we could go back the next day," Rob explained, "have the owner check the keg, and say, 'See? It's working!'"

Self-delivery put them in direct contact with taverns, and they would do anything to pick up a handle. Kurt describes one particularly intractable contact, the now-defunct Rusty Pelican. "After working that angle forever, he finally said, 'Okay, but I'm not going to give you one of my beer taps. You have to use this wine tap.' It hadn't been used for several years and it wasn't refrigerated and it was grotty as hell." They had to clean it and install a CO_2 line just to make it work—and they were happy to do it.

Unfortunately, their salesmanship couldn't alter the fact that drinkers just weren't taking to Altbier. "It really wasn't selling," said Kurt. "We had several accounts that *wanted* it to sell, but it just wasn't. Like Rob said, we thought it needed to be radically different, but we overestimated where the market would be."

"We needed to do something," Rob said. "We were only brewing something like a couple times a month, if that." The descendants of farmers, they had arranged to sell spent grain to their cousin to feed his pigs, and they weren't even brewing enough for him.

Things had become dire. The brewery, which was undercapitalized to begin with, wasn't brewing enough beer to meet expenses. By midsummer of 1985, Rob and Kurt were just weeks from bankruptcy unless they came up with a new plan. They thought maybe they should introduce another beer. As homebrewers, they had made a wheat beer that was popular with friends—perhaps that would sell better than Altbier. Well, they had to try something.

HEFEWEIZEN

THE ALTBIER ERA LASTED ABOUT FIVE MONTHS. KURT and Rob did yeomen's work trying to sell their sole beer, but as the weeks wore on, it became clear that Portland just wasn't charmed by their dark, bitter ale. Given the pace of modern product releases, it's remarkable they stuck with the beer so long, but they had invested a great deal of time and money—and, even more importantly, emotion—in their identity as an altbier brewery. Moving on from that vision took time.

Eventually, they had to consider other beers. But before you jump to any conclusions, the new era—which lasted nearly a year—was *not* the beer that made the brewery famous. Well, not exactly.

FIRST, THERE WAS WEIZEN

The second beer introduced by Widmer Brewing was a light, clear wheat beer called Weizen. They continued to make Altbier, but decided to call up this beer from Kurt's homebrewing portfolio. "We brewed it and had been drinking it," Rob said. "We liked Weizen and introduced it because we realized people wanted something a little more approachable." In addition to looking like the familiar golden lager people were used to drinking, it had half the bitterness of Altbier.

Weizen was brewed to the same recipe and formulation as their future flagship, Hefeweizen, but Weizen went through the additional stage of filtration. At the time, it would have never occurred to Rob and Kurt to offer it unfiltered—beer was always bright and sparkling. In fact, they had learned that any beer that wasn't perfectly clear raised red flags. "Our filtration was so rudimentary," Rob explained, "that frequently the Alt or the Weizen would have a haze, and people immediately thought it was bad. Our experience was that cloudy beer was bad, negative." Americans knew so little about beer that they had trouble assessing the new craft beers, but clarity seemed like an obvious marker. Already suspicious that little breweries were making unsafe or unclean beer, haze seemed to confirm that this was little more than fermented moonshine. So the Widmers filtered and filtered.

They named it Weizen because their branding cast back to the German tradition that inspired them, but it wasn't much like the wheat beers made in Germany. The traditional weizens (pronounced *VITE-sin*) are made in Bavaria, far from Düsseldorf, and are characterized by a particular yeast strain. In the classic profile, those yeasts produce assertive flavors of banana and clove. But the Widmers weren't trying to allude to that beer when they named their own wheat beer Weizen—it's just the German word for wheat.

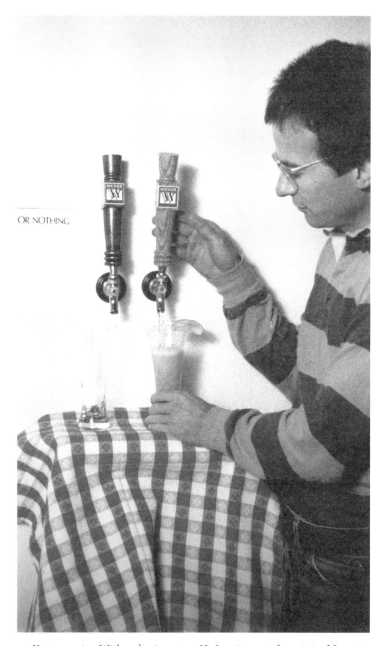

OR NOTHING

Kurt pouring Widmer's signature Hefeweizen at the original Lovejoy brewery, in front of what they called the "Wall of Eternal Beer."

Pronunciations

Kurt and Rob have always been scrupulous in the German pronunciation of their flagship beer: *HAY-fuh-VITE-sin*. Oregonians were … less so. They invariably pronounced it *heffa-wise-un*. After decades of effort, the brewery started using a shorthand, Hefe, hoping to convince people to pronounce at least half the word correctly. (The jury's still out.) For some reason, Oregonians also reliably mispronounce the brewery's name, which *is* phonetical. In Oregon, you almost always hear people say *Widmeer*. So for decades, Rob and Kurt have been patiently listening to their customers order "Widmeer heffa-wise-un."

Despite their German names, Weizen and Hefeweizen are classically American beers. This is the central truth at the root of the entire Widmer Brothers story, one that explains the beer's early popularity, Widmer's massive growth, and why Hefeweizen remains one of the most popular beers in America. The names have always created some level of confusion because of this—the brewery has tried to qualify Hefe as an "American Hefeweizen," among other appellations—but make no mistake, nearly everything about the wheaty ales bears the hallmarks of American DNA.

We need to step back a moment and consider what "American" (or "German," for that matter) even means. Have you ever stopped to consider why different beer styles developed in different parts of the world? Why cask ales flourished in England and pilsners are prized in the Czech Republic? The phenomenon has repeated itself countless times throughout beer's long history. For reasons specific (availability of local ingredients, brewing philosophy, social habits of consumers, even things like war and tax law) and reasons mysterious (the unexplainable force of culture), local populations gravitate to distinctive kinds of beer.

It's why the citizens of Düsseldorf choose to drink that dark, bitter ale, altbier, to the exclusion of all other styles, but in Cologne, a half hour down the Rhine, the locals won't touch it. Their local style is kölsch, a pale, less bitter ale. And back in Düsseldorf, good luck finding the pale beers of Cologne. It's impossible to explain why this happens; it just does. As beer culture deepens, people develop collective tastes. Counterintuitively, the more mature a place's beer culture, the more restricted the choices of beer.

Rob and Kurt had already run up against one of those mysterious cultural barriers: the American palate, whatever it would one day become, did not seem to favor altbier. But although it wouldn't fully emerge for a couple decades, it turns out there is a distinctly American palate, and Hefeweizen, despite its name, had all the classically American qualities we now prize.

But we're getting ahead of the story. At first, the Widmers were only offering an alternative to Altbier, something that would get the kettle boiling again, and Weizen was just the ticket. "It picked up right away," Kurt

258 - Pale
250 - wheat
35 - Munich
15 - crystal

Weizenbier

O.G. ⋟ 11-12% (44-48)
BU ⋟ 12-18   (compares to 28-40 BUs for Altbier)
   Grain combination 60 % pale
                      40 % wheat
                      (5% crystal)? To emphasize maltiness

Mash - optimally ⋟ mash in at 99°F + raise temp to
122° in 20 minutes

   45 min. protein rest at 122°-126°
   30 min @ 154°
   To conversion @ 158°

Boil - 120 min

Fermentation - ① Temp 64°-71° until 2% (S6.8) fermentable remain
   ② Beer pumped to next tank + lagered 3-4 days @ 53
   ③ Beer pumped to next tank (Bright Beer Tank) and
   lagered 7-14 days @ 32°-36°

50°C 122-124°F : 30 min. → stir 5 min intervals
62°C 144°F : 20 min
70°C 158°F : 10-20 min
77°C 170°F : mash off / sparge
        Temp rise 1°C/min.

        530
        ~~525~~ lbs. pale
        30 lbs. crystal
        30 lbs Munich
        10 lbs Roast
        600 lbs.
            O.G. = 46
            F.E. = 10-12

alt/water   mash in 600 lbs grain / ~~180~~ gal. H$_2$O
: 2 -   144-150
1 2.5   sparge · 150 gal.

            3.5 - 3.7 oz. Calcium Sulfate ≈ 80 ppm.

                                start
            Fermentation temp 59°F (15°C) → 68-71°F (20-22°C)

            Perle   - 7.9 lbs
            Tettnanger - 3.4 lbs.

            3.6 oz Calcium Sulfate

The original Weizenbier recipe sheet.

said. "We went from two batches a week to two batches a day in very short order." People remember the launch of Altbier because it was such an important early beer in Oregon, and they recall Hefeweizen's dramatic arrival, but Weizen is often written out of the history. Yet it was a success on its own merits.

Rob tells a story that captures how people responded when Widmer released it: "One of my favorite recollections is with the old Produce Row. Steve Turnsten was the guy who ran it. I remember going in the front door and he was sitting down inside. I poured him a pint and he drank the whole pint and he said, 'I'm gonna sell the *shit* out of this.' Produce Row was the spot back then. And he did, man—he just cruised."

Weizen may have had a German name, but when you look at the early surviving recipes, it looks pretty American. A grain bill consisted of about 45 percent wheat malt, along with American pale malt, Munich malt, and crystal malts ("to emphasize maltiness" is written in notes for an earlier batch). The use of American 2-row malt here was a response to availability, but it's one of those elements that led to a more American taste. German pilsner malt has a more distinctive, grainy flavor, while American barley is neutral, accentuating the flavor of wheat in the beer.

They originally used a more classic German mash schedule, but later simplified it. Interestingly, the first mash schedule they used would have produced the clove flavor characteristic of Bavarian wheat beers—*if* they had used a Bavarian yeast strain. The altbier strain, however, fermented clean, so fermentation flavors were absent, again putting the focus on wheat. Where things start to look very American was in their hopping schedule. In a 1986 recipe, in which they were doing a long, two-hour boil, it looked like this. The times listed are the minutes before the end of the boil.

- 3 LBS TETTNANGER 105 MINUTES
- 3 LBS TETTNANGER 60 MINUTES
- 1 LB CASCADE 3 MINUTES
- 1 LB TETTNANGER (HOP JACK)

I have seen a number of German recipes for a number of different ale styles, and I have never seen hops added as late as three minutes before the end of boil (if brewers want some aromatics, the latest they'll go is 10-15 minutes before the end of boil). The hop jack is a separate vessel used to infuse the wort with hops after it has been taken off the boil, much like you'd make tea. I have *never* seen a German brewer use this technique. Those two later additions are used to pull the flavors and aromas from hops, rather than bitterness. It is typical in English brewing to have this kind of hop schedule, and it has become almost ubiquitous in American brewing.

US Tettnanger

Tettnang, Germany, is a traditional hop-growing region, and the famous, ancient landrace hop grown there is named for it. Decades ago, Americans planted that hop in the Pacific Northwest (possibly from a Swiss cultivar), but somewhere along the line there was a mistake. Eventually, experts began to question the source of the hop sold as US Tettnanger, concluding that it was probably more closely related to Fuggle, an English hop. Care to guess what other hops are descended from Fuggle? Willamette and Cascade, two indelible American varieties that rewrote brewing here. When Rob and Kurt made their first batches of Weizen with Tettnanger, they were shooting for a German character. What they got instead was probably more American than they realized. Weizen is now made entirely with American hops.

It's no wonder Kurt and Rob decided to add a layer of hopping to this beer. It was a simple ale that took flavor from the wheat and crystal malts, but little else. Hops were used to give it a floral, spritzy flavor and increase its complexity. When you look at those early recipes, what you see is far less a Bavarian weissbier than something much more familiar to Americans: a pale ale, albeit one made with wheat malt. Given where the craft beer trends would take us, it's no wonder people responded to Weizen.

However, as popular as Weizen seemed to Rob and Kurt in 1985, nothing could have prepared them for what would happen the next year.

THE BIRTH OF THE HAZE

If there is a creation myth for Widmer Brothers, it happened on May 15, 1986. But unlike most myths, this one's actually true. Whatever fuzziness remains results from fading memories and the loss of the central figure, Carl Simpson, who owned the Dublin Pub on Southeast Belmont. Carl was a champion of local breweries and was trying to assemble groups of three beers from each of the extant locals at the time. Here's where the story picks up.

KURT: "Carl would say, 'Both your beers are doing great.' And then he said, 'Can you do a third beer?' With two fermenters it wasn't possible to do. So one day it's like, well, let's just take the beer straight out of the lagering tank and not run it through the filter."

ROB: "And we knew about kristalweizen [a filtered wheat beer] and hefeweizen [a cloudy version]—that was kind of the idea."

KURT: "It was not really a batch of Hefe, it was just Weizen. I have the kegging log that shows that when we were kegging that batch, we bypassed filtration and just went direct to keg, and those are the ones that went to the Dublin Pub. So there isn't really a Hefe recipe. Some we filtered, and some we didn't, and that was Hefe.

"But it's important to note that this was 1986 and nobody had seen a beer that looked like that. They were accustomed to the Weizen and were enjoying that. We were worried about our reputation, we were worried about the impression it was going to make to somebody who was having their first Widmer look like that. So it was only supposed to be for Dublin Pub.

WIDMER BREWING COMPANY
MATERIALS IN-PROCESS FORM

No. 86 113

DATE STARTED: 6-2 ,19 86   DATE ENDED: _____,198__
BEER TYPE: Alt   MAT. REQ.#: _____
QUANTITY (BARRELS): N   JOB#: 113

TRANSFERRED TO FINISHED GOODS (BARRELS): _____

TYPE	QUANTITY
PALE	540
WHEAT	
CRYSTAL 40L	45
MUNICH	40
ROAST	10
HALLERTAUER	
PERLE	5.5
TETTNANG	3
CASCADE	
IRISH MOSS	40z

COMMENTS: _____

~~THL THL THL~~
~~THL THL II~~

145° starting temp

11:35   Boil
11:50   2# Perle
12:20   3.5# Perle
12:50   4 oz Irish Moss
1:17   2# tett
1:20   End boil

2# tett   hop back

Mash in   45 min   134°
Raise to 144° 20 min
Raise to 158Clow

	OG	44
6-3	56	38
6-4	56	24
6-5	56	13

WIDMER BREWING COMPANY
MATERIALS IN-PROCESS FORM   No. 86 112

DATE STARTED: _5-30_____,19 86 DATE ENDED: _____,198 86
BEER TYPE: _Weizen_____   MAT. REQ.#: __8141___
QUANTITY (BARRELS): __10_____ JOB#: __112___

TRANSFERRED TO FINISHED GOODS (BARRELS): _____

TYPE	QUANTITY
PALE	270
WHEAT	270
CRYSTAL 40ℓ	15
MUNICH	40
ROAST	
HALLERTAUER	
PERLE	
TETTNANG	7
CASCADE	1
IRISH MOSS	4oz

COMMENTS:

꒼꒼꒼ ꒼꒼ III +10

꒼꒼꒼ ꒼꒼ III +10

Ambient Temp 75°F
Starting Temp 144°F
2.5oz @ SO₄ to Mash

Mash in at
~~Starting Temp~~ 124°F

11:35 Boil
11:50 3# Tett
12:35 3# Tett
1:05   4oz Irish Moss
1:32   1# Cascade
1:35   End Boil

      1# Tett hop jack

      OG 42
5-31 SG 37
6-1   SG 22

┌─────────────────────┐
│   Lager Tank   │
│ 5-31 SG 18   │
│ 6-1   SG 14   │
│ 6-2   SG 12   │
└─────────────────────┘

Altbier and Weizen brew sheets.

"The great thing was, Carl was the first account in Portland who had the big weizenbier glasses. And the Hefeweizen looked great in those with a lemon on the side. So Carl had waitstaff just load up a tray and walk around. It's so great that we were in Portland—people would look at that and go, 'What is that?' and Carl would tell them, 'You gotta try it,' and they would."

ROB: "I guess Carl was the one who started the lemon thing. Carl was already doing that with our Weizen. When we went with Hefe, it just stuck.

"It was so unusual. I have another vivid memory there in the Dublin Pub. It was a Friday night and I was sitting at the bar with Carl, and he said, 'I'm going to do something here. Watch what happens—this is incredible.' He was already using the half-liter weizenbier glasses, so he filled up the four glasses, garnished them with lemon, put them on a tray, and had the waitress just walk around. It's an intimate place but as she walked through people's conversations stopped. You could see they were processing: what was *that*? People would look at the tray, they would point, and then by midnight everyone was drinking it. The appearance was just mind-blowing and that got people interested in having a taste, and once they tasted it they loved it. By midnight everybody had one of those half-liters of Hefe in front of them."

KURT: "The end of the story is that it was a popular after-hours place for other bar managers and owners around Portland. He told them, 'It is unbelievable the volumes we're selling of this.' So people would call us, and the first few calls we tried to talk them out of it. I mean, really. Being the smart guys that we are and all. And then we couldn't make enough.

"That was the thing—the weizenbier was just a bitch to filter, and once Hefe really started to go, we were like, 'This is the greatest thing in the world!' We could go right out of the tank and into the kegs; it saved us a *day*. Filtering ten barrels of Weizen was ridiculous, and all of a sudden—boom!—didn't need to."

By the time Carl Simpson started selling glasses of that first keg of Hefeweizen, Kurt and Rob had been making beer for a year and a half. In all that time, it was an article of faith that beer had to be clear. They'd already learned from Altbier that if they made something too weird, it just wouldn't sell. It's evident from their accounts of this moment that they had no reason to believe Hefeweizen was on the right side of that equation. They were just trying to give an important account one more beer.

In fact, the billowing cloudiness turned out to be a huge asset *because* it was so obviously intentional. It caught people's attention and intrigued them enough to give it a try. But unlike the aggressively bitter Altbier, Hefeweizen had a light, delicate flavor profile. The beer looked strange, but it tasted just familiar enough that people were quick converts.

The lemon slice was another stroke of genius—or was it luck? Those early days of craft brewing involved a fair number of gimmicks as breweries tried to lure drinkers into sampling their beer, but unlike the honey and berries some breweries used, the lemon had a hidden logic when it garnished a Widmer Hefeweizen. It created a perfect visual cue—an inducement for those initially put off by the cloudiness—for the lightly spritzy ale infused with citrusy-floral American hops. Even for the people, and there were many of them, who immediately plucked the lemon wedge off the glass's rim, the impression of citrus carried through to the beer itself.

The Lemon Question

"The lemon is controversial," Kurt acknowledges. "Where I lived in Germany, it wasn't even until the 1990s that there was draft hefeweizen. So where I lived the lemon was by request. My German brother-in-law claims it was only for weizen but never hefeweizen. I don't have that recollection. If you ordered it, they took the weizen glass and the lemon round and trapped it in the bottom of the glass, and then they inverted the glass over the bottle and turned the whole thing back around and slowly bring the bottle up. You had to request the lemon."

This turned out to be Hefeweizen's secret weapon: the combination of a shocking appearance followed by a light, approachable flavor profile. For months and months, Rob and Kurt had been trying to break through and reach customers, and Hefeweizen's presentation finally did it. The tall glass topped with a lemon slice became its own advertisement, and in pub after pub, the word started spreading. "That's an example of how Portland was such a fantastic market to start," Kurt recalled. "Most people would look at the cloudiness and say, 'So?' Not immediately jumping to the conclusion that there's a problem, but: 'Let me try it.'"

Of course, not everyone was drawn to the appearance. Rob's wife Barb tells the story of the first time she saw Hefeweizen in Heppner, a little town in Eastern Oregon, in 1993. Her story, amusing as it is, shows where the market for most beer drinkers was in those early days: the vast majority were perfectly happy with their sparkling lager and weren't looking for anything new.

"Actually, the most dramatic memory I have is about three weeks after I met Rob, he took me out and said, 'I want you to have a Widmer Hefeweizen.' And he put down this beer, and it was this cloudy stuff, and I was looking at it like 'What the hell?' I was thinking, 'Do I tell him his beer is defective?' I mean, I had no idea. Finally, I'm like, 'What's wrong with your beer?' He said, 'Nothing; it's supposed to be that way.' I was a Coors Light drinker—I didn't even know what a microbrewery was. No idea." A few years later, after they were married, her grandmother was introduced to the beer and suggested Rob "use a little potato" to clear it up.

Kurt tells a similar story of what happened once they traveled outside Portland. "There were markets, I can't even remember—Texas?—where people wouldn't even try a sample. It hadn't occurred to us that, you're in a bar, people are drinking beer, and you'd say, 'Would you like to sample my beer?' And for someone to say no—that was a whole new world for me. I mean in Portland it's like, 'Of course I would! A free sample? Give it to me!' They'd knock you down to get it. When we got to markets where people didn't want a free sample? I mean, we weren't advertising on TV, we didn't have half-naked women; it was all sampling. And when people *wouldn't even try it*, then I'm dead in the water. Where do you go from there?"

Fortunately, the brewery did start in Portland. Enough adventuresome drinkers were willing to try Hefeweizen that it soon began to consume all of their attention. "We were so out of beer for so many years," Rob said, a little ruefully. They would begin to expand in a few years, adding new breweries and finally moving to a bigger facility, but from the first deliveries of Hefeweizen in 1986 until they built their final, enormous brewery on North Russell Street, trying to meet demand just looked like triage.

Beer Moves in Mysterious Ways

Hefeweizen didn't become popular overnight, despite its showy debut. One element of the story old-timers recall is how the beer became popular with bartenders who would retire to the Dublin Pub for a nightcap.

They started drinking Hefeweizen, and pretty soon they were making sure it was pouring at their bars, too.

Morgan Miller, who worked as a bartender in the 1980s before going on to work for several Oregon breweries, recalls one of the main reasons for the beer's popularity: "The Dublin Pub was one of the four or five craft places that would stay open until closing time, two-thirty," he said. "Between the Barley Mill, the East Avenue, the Horse Brass, and some other place—maybe the Belmont Inn?—the Dublin Pub was the one place where all the bartenders could meet up with their girlfriends. All our girlfriends started drinking this Hefeweizen stuff, and we all wanted our girlfriends at *our* bar drinking that beer, not at somebody *else's* bar drinking it."

Rob described a typical day. "Our drivers would come in and we'd have these discussions on the dock: 'Okay, Produce Row's got enough beer to get them through 'til Friday, and Dublin's going to need it, so they get it.' And somebody else would say, 'Oh, I just delivered to Tavern and Pool, so they're not going to need it until Saturday, so I'll go get one from there and take it over here.' It was ridiculous; kegs would come off the line and go right on the truck."

The initial brewery had a maximum capacity of about 9,000 barrels, which even by today's standards is a lot of beer. (It's more than two million of those lemon-wedged pints.) In today's market, a brewery that size would be in

Ray checking the fill level of the whirlpool tank.

the top 20 percent of all craft breweries. In the mid-1980s, it made Widmer one of the most successful breweries in the country.

THE BEER THAT BUILT BEERVANA

If you glance at a list of the largest American craft breweries, one thing jumps out: they all have an enormously popular flagship beer. Sam Adams, Boston Lager; Sierra Nevada, Pale Ale; New Belgium, Fat Tire; and the list goes on, through Lagunitas, Deschutes, Bell's, Founders, and Stone. But only a few of those beers have had anywhere near the influence of Widmer's Hefeweizen, a beer with at least three important bullet points under its legacy.

The first: in a few short years, it transformed Portland into a craft beer mecca. It's true that there was some early buzz about craft beer in the 1980s, but despite newspaper articles and television news stories, few people were actually drinking the stuff. And yet by 1994, *Willamette Week* had coined the moniker "Beervana" to refer to Portland. In less than a decade's time, a wave of breweries had opened up, and craft beer had gone from the margins to the mainstream. Oregon has always far outpaced the rest of the United States in terms of craft beer adoption, and our awakening happened a decade earlier than the rest of the country. (Chicago and San Francisco didn't become decent beer cities until well into the new century. New York's still not.) A single reason never accounts for any broad cultural change, but Widmer Hefeweizen probably deserves the lion's share of the credit for Oregon's speedy transformation.

It's hard to over-emphasize just how popular Hefeweizen was from the late 1980s through the next decade. The overall beer market was bigger than it had ever been in America. Drinkers were curious about craft beers (or "microbrews," as they were known at the time), and they needed a place to start. Even by the late 1980s, the proliferation of names and styles was already underway, which made it confusing for people dipping their toes in the craft waters. People weren't sure whether they should focus on the brewery, the style, or specific beers, and they'd make halting attempts when ordering pints. Hefeweizen arrived at the perfect moment. It had an unmistakable appearance and an unusual but familiar flavor. People could readily identify it, and once they managed to wrap their mouths around the word "Hefeweizen," they always knew what to order. For a large percentage of the drinking population, Hefeweizen *was* microbrew.

Before his death, local beer legend Fred Eckhardt, who'd been writing about beer since the 1960s, told Brian Yaeger of *Willamette Week*, "[Hefeweizen] revolutionized the craft-beer availability in town. It had flavor as an alternate to Bud, Coors, Miller." It was so popular that every pub and restaurant wanted to have it on tap for people who wanted a micro, and anyone who had micros on tap wanted the one beer everyone knew. That feedback loop was not only good for the Widmers; it also helped push craft into places it would have otherwise taken years or decades to reach. Stuart Ramsay, the pub manager for rival BridgePort, was never a giant fan of the beer, but nevertheless conceded, "Hefeweizen was a really important beer. In terms of the beer culture and what happened here, a *very* important beer."

Sanjay Reddy is a Portland writer who documents beer on his *Not So Professional Beer Blog*, and his story is typical of the mental transition people went through once they made first contact with Hefeweizen. "In the mid-'90s, I lived in Illinois, a craft beer wasteland. If you wanted a beer in the Land of Lincoln, your choices were macro. I chose to avoid beer entirely. Around this time, I visited Portland for the first time on a business trip. While at dinner, one of my coworkers suggested I taste a local beer. I asked the server to surprise me, and she brought back a tall, curvy glass filled with what appeared to be orange juice. She told me it was a beer called Hefeweizen. With a few sips, the seeds of my beer journey were planted. Widmer Hefeweizen has always held a special place in my heart because it was my first good beer. It was unlike anything I ever tasted."

Of course, that popularity led to imitators—the second bullet point under Hefeweizen's legacy. Without really intending to, the Widmers had invented a style of beer that would become ubiquitous across the Northwest. One of the early competitors was Hart Brewing (later known as Pyramid), located just across the Columbia, about forty miles north of Portland, in Kalama, Washington. Like Widmer, Pyramid followed up their debut with a wheat beer, which they called Wheaten Ale, in 1985. It was successful, but not on the scale of Widmer Hefeweizen. In 1993, they decided to rebrand it as Pyramid Hefeweizen, and then it became a popular rival—and one, Kurt and Rob noted with growing anxiety, available in a bottle.

Because there was such a strong connection between micro and hefeweizen, most other Northwest breweries had to brew their own versions. Then, in the mid-1990s, a brewery speculator named Jim Bernau planned a brewery in Portland to add to a national network he wanted to build. He hired Karl Ockert away from BridgePort to brew beer for the newly minted Nor'Wester Brewery. Karl recounted how they decided which beers to brew: "Jim Bernau was looking and going, 'What's the most popular style of beer? Wheat beer. That's what we're going to make.' So we made our own hefeweizen, and we did quite well with it. And then, because Berry Weizen [actually called Widberry, another Widmer product] was big, we made a Raspberry Weizen. It was awful beer, but it did quite well." Indeed it did; at one time, Nor'Wester's hefeweizen was the best-selling bottled beer in Oregon.

People who knew about the German beer were confused about the Northwest's hefeweizen, which didn't taste much like the Bavarian original. Garrett Oliver, master brewer for Brooklyn Brewing, told the *New York Times* that the Widmers were "trading on the good name of an actual, established style to sell something that's different. It's confusing and frustrating." His comment may not have been entirely innocent—at the time, he was promoting his own Brooklyner Weisse, a classic Bavarian-style weizen—but it wasn't unusual.

Kurt at the hopjack.

And Northwesterners who knew about Widmer were confused when they came across a Bavarian version. Portland Brewing actually made one of those—Uncle Otto's—but nobody would buy it in Oregon, so they sold it mainly in the Chicago market. Some of the most famous beer styles emerge when a brewery or region riffs on an existing style but makes them "wrong" (that's how we got pilsners). The Widmers were responsible for inventing a style, even if it did offend traditionalists.

The third bullet point is the most important of Hefeweizen's legacies, and the one Widmer Brothers least often gets credit for. Despite the name and the lemon wedge and the reputation for being a "crossover" beer, it goes back to the question of DNA: Widmer Hefeweizen helped create the qualities we now consider archetypal in American beer. In retrospect, it was, as Rob has admitted on many occasions, "a wheat pale ale." But more than that, it had the characteristics we now consider mandatory in American ales:

- CLOUDINESS AND RUSTICITY: In 1986, Hefeweizen's cloudiness was the most potent rebuke to industrial lagers Portlanders had ever seen. In later years, haziness became associated with the addition of bales of hops, and many drinkers regard an IPA with skepticism if it doesn't have at least a shimmer of haze. In Oregon, drinkers started associating "cloudy" with "artisanal" and "flavorful."
- LATE HOP FLAVORS: This goes back to those three-minute and hop-jack additions Rob and Kurt made to Weizen in 1984. They infused the beer with a lovely

floral aroma and gave it that citrusy zing. Those qualities are now such a huge part of the American tradition that even lagers regularly feature them.

- ◆ DRINKABILITY: It wasn't always obvious that Americans would land on beers that could be drunk in twos and threes, particularly when they were crazy for very bitter, very alcoholic beers. The evolution away from bitterness and toward hop flavors and aromas has to do with the shift toward pub beers. Everything about Widmer Hefeweizen—from the light, fluffy mouthfeel to the citrus undertones to the crisp finish—was engineered for drinking in session, at a pub or on the back porch.

In a blog post written after he visited Oregon, Stan Hieronymus was surprised to find the beers were typically cloudy. "In fact, we've seen plenty of hazy beers in Oregon (not just the ones made with wheat). I guess there is a pun in there about 'partly cloudy,' but I'll pass. ... On a per capita basis there's a lot more haze in Oregon." He also noted their focus on hops and their toothsome drinkability, but it was the cloudiness that seemed unusual. As always, Oregon was quietly way ahead of the pack—and Widmer Hefeweizen was a big reason Oregonians got used to the clouds before everyone else.

Drinkers can develop all kinds of different preferences, and it's impossible to guess why they choose altbier over witbier, pilsner over Irish stout. The process is organic and always particular to the place where the beer is made. Now well into the second decade of the new century, we can map the preferences of Americans to the beers we drink. When you strip Widmer Hefeweizen of its funny German name, forget its long history, and settle in with a pint, you'll find those qualities we consider "modern" were there all along. Hefeweizen was one of the key beers in establishing the Northwest palate, which was just a decade or three ahead of where America finally landed, too.

MOVING UP, TO RUSSELL STREET AND BEYOND

I REMEMBER THE FIRST TIME I VISITED B. MOLOCH, THE signature Portland restaurant of the 1980s and an offshoot of the Heathman. Founding chef Greg Higgins introduced locals to the kind of food the rest of the country now associates with the city: farm-fresh and seasonal, highlighting the bounty of Oregon's fields, pastures, and seas. It was a bright, sunny day, and golden light suffused the restaurant. The Widmers had contracted with Heathman to install a ten-barrel brewery in a corner of the place, effectively turning it into a brewpub. It was Portland's first experiment with haute cuisine and craft beer, and it gave us an early inkling of the potential of the two as dance partners. (Higgins, a beer geek before there was a term for such a thing, would go on to establish the restaurant bearing his name with a beer list running for pages.) The year was 1990.

Kurt and Rob load the "pride of the fleet" off the dock at the Russell Street brewery.

At that point I was already well familiar with Hefeweizen, and I suspect I ordered something more obscure. Nevertheless, when I looked around the room, a substantial majority of diners had tall, hazy glasses in front of them. They must have outnumbered wine glasses four or five to one. This was not the first brew-pub in town by a longshot, but it arrived at the moment Hefeweizen was establishing itself as the city beer—an impressive feat with Blitz-Weinhard just a few blocks north. As such, going there was like visiting the future. The food was unusual and special, and the beer, which seemed to glow from within its hazy center, was other-worldly. Portland was transitioning into the artisanal era that would make it famous for everything from handmade chocolate to hand-roasted coffee. There were a few quintessential institutions that made that transition inevitable, and on that summer day, I knew I was sitting in one of them.

SMITHSON AND MCKAY

That day I visited B. Moloch came during heady times for the Widmers. The success of Hefeweizen had led to nonstop growth, which led to a kind of triage to increase production. First came the expansion into downtown and B. Moloch's. "They approached us because brewpubs were the coming thing," Kurt recalled. "We needed more capacity. They wanted to do Portland's first upscale brewpub, and it was the Heathman Group, so everything was very tasteful, very elegant." Being associated with the Heathman and having a downtown location were both excellent decisions. Hefeweizen was already available across the city, from working-class taverns to corner pubs and restaurants. Being placed in a Heathman restaurant exposed the brand to a steady clientele of upscale drinkers.

But the solution to the capacity problem almost immediately became a new capacity problem. This would be the case for the first ten-plus years of Widmer Brothers' existence, during which the company would ultimately construct four breweries. Every time Kurt and Rob made a decision about expanding, they underestimated the potential growth and found themselves almost immediately confronting another expansion. "We built a second brewery of the same size downtown," Kurt recounted, "and then we outgrew both of those." By the late 1980s—five years after launching—they were on the hunt for their third brewery. The rapid growth brought with it a sense of vertigo and offered little time for reflection.

Had they stopped to consider their mid- to long-term trajectory, Rob and Kurt might have gotten dizzy. The difficulty of planning for the future is trying to guess which variables will come into play. The Widmers certainly couldn't have predicted the effect Hefeweizen was going to have on the Pacific Northwest. The future is dynamic, and Hefeweizen's success was busy shaping it. I wasn't the only one who visited B. Moloch to glimpse the future. Competitors came in droves, and they all took notes.

In 1988, however, the success of that beer presented itself in the form of a single, all-consuming question: how do we make more? To answer it, the Widmers started to look for a space where they could install a much larger brewery, which they thought would handle not just current but future growth. They went out on a search for an appropriate building, ultimately looking at sixty or more possible sites.

They kept coming back to a place they'd known about for years, just off North Interstate Avenue and north of the Broadway Bridge. It was formerly the home of the Storefront Theater on North Russell, and a friend of their father Ray had a shop in the building. The site actually contained two buildings, anchoring the business district in what was originally the separate town of Albina. An intact little neighborhood sat just behind the buildings, but overhead, the dull thunder of traffic rumbled from

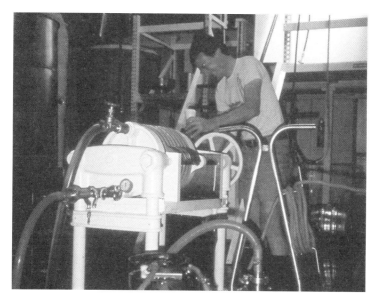

Kurt at the original filter.

a tangle of highway overpasses. It was centrally located, just a couple miles from downtown, but on the edge of a massive industrial preserve that stretched to Swan Island. Yet on the other side were miles of neighborhoods in Northeast Portland slowly undergoing a revival—and quite likely thirsty for a good beer.

Known as the Smithson and McKay Brothers Block in the National Register of Historic Places, the buildings were built in 1890 and 1893. The Smithson building, on the corner of Russell and Interstate, is in the Romanesque Revival style; the McKay is Italian Renaissance. They come from an era of optimism and efficiency—not ornate, but spacious and well-designed. The lower commercial story had broad, welcoming windows that seemed to say, "We're open for business."

The first time Kurt and Rob considered Smithson and McKay, they decided it was too big. It had also fallen on hard times, reflecting a turn from eighty years earlier. The brick had blackened and some of the windows were boarded up. Its historic designation made it a commercial albatross because no one wanted to buy a building in that part of town that they couldn't strip bare. But, as they sold more and more beer, they kept coming back to Smithson and McKay.

The Widmers began to consider the site a real possibility, but in 1988, the Portland City Council was preparing to approve a buyer who would have leveled the building. At the last moment, the Widmers managed to swing a deal to take over the property. They didn't even have to pay for the building—just the land it sat on—as long as they agreed to properly rehab it. So, in September of 1988, they took ownership of their third brewery.

Russell Street Rehab

The story of the buildings that now house the pub and offices could be expanded to a book of its own. This exchange gives some sense of what an all-consuming project it was for literally years.

KURT: "So we kept coming back to this brewery because it looked like a brewpub and a brewery. And it was [dramatic pause] ... free. Free! We had to buy the land that it sits on. It was effectively condemned. The owner had gone bankrupt; the bank owned it.

There was a proposal to demolish it. What saved it was its spot on the National Historic Registry. A building that's on the Registry can only be demolished with unanimous consent of the City Council. At the eleventh hour, we came in with a rehab proposal rather than a demo proposal, and so we trumped the other guy. But the building was not in very good condition. All the wooden storefronts were rotted out. Boarded up. Pigeon shit on everything. The roof on the far building leaked and had for some time so there was lots of rot. There had been a fire in the roof."

ROB: "When we moved into this building, we had a construction crew. And those guys—it was later I realized it, but I think they thought they'd died and gone to heaven. We're not concerned with how long it's going to take or how much it's going to cost, but we just want it done well. So we ended up with all these craftsmen who were making beautiful pieces of the building. They were on the payroll. We were paying them payroll and workers' comp. We joked, 'We should change it to Widmer Construction.'"

Taking over the Smithson and McKay buildings was an enormous commitment, but it reflected the brothers' optimism for the future. Because financing continued to be a challenge, most craft breweries were established in marginal buildings and used provisional equipment. These buildings were historic, dating back to the early days of the city. Once renovated, they would be an impressive sight. In archival footage shot not long after they acquired the building, Rob and Kurt express a candid ambition:

"This feels like a brewery," Rob says. "It feels like home. I just look forward to having the brewery here, the pub here. I really see this becoming a landmark in Portland. There isn't going to be anything like it—in Portland or Seattle."

Kurt agrees. "One of the things that sold me most on this building was the way it's positioned here in this geographical area; it makes a statement about Widmer Brewing Company."

It would take years to complete—and ultimately cost as much as a new building—but it would become the landmark they envisioned. They installed a thirty-barrel brewhouse to replace the original dairy equipment kit on Lovejoy. They sold the first brewery but kept the small one downtown, allowing them to nearly triple production, begin meeting orders again, and start expanding.

HIRING A CEO

There was just one problem: before long, they realized the new brewery wasn't big enough, either. Orders kept pouring in, and within a few short years they were right back where they started: trying to figure out how to meet demand. Kurt groans when he thinks back on this time.

"I was always overly cautious," he said. "The second brewery we built should have been bigger than the first one. This one should have been ten times bigger than the first one, and instead it was thirty barrels."

Members of the early Widmer team.

Of course, present-day Kurt knows a lot more than 1990 Kurt did. Widmer had continually grown faster than expectations—it was by then a midsized brewery—but there was no guarantee it would continue to grow. Up until that point, the brothers had been able to merely scale up in order to grow. The business, though larger, was fundamentally the same operation. But as the brewery started outgrowing its new confines, something changed. Sebastian Pastore, the young Reed graduate who was quickly becoming a trusted leader, described the situation. "Kurt [then CEO] had gotten to the point that he was overwhelmed. He had to make every decision himself and he didn't have anyone he could turn to. Sales and marketing and delivery and quality and brewing and all the stuff really came directly to him without any structure." If the company were going to continue to grow, it would have to evolve into something new.

Moments of expansion are a difficult time for any company. Widmer Brewing was on the cusp of transitioning from a small, highly integrated company where the owners could pull all the levers of control, to a larger, more diffuse one that would require additional management. "[Small] companies often just don't have a lot of systems and structure," Pastore explained. "They're just making it up as they go along. We certainly didn't have strategic plans for five years." On one hand, if they decided to grow, the brewery would evolve into a fundamentally different organization. It would mean giving control of parts of the business to someone else. On the other hand, the business couldn't grow if Kurt and Rob continued to oversee everything.

Kurt's wife, Ann, a professor in the School of Management at Concordia University, was a presence during all of the brewery's important transitions. She remembers this decision point vividly. "What they did at that point was recognize, correctly, that they didn't know it all," she told me. "But they didn't have huge egos. [That's what] tends to sink entrepreneurs. They can't let go of their concept, or they can't recognize that they don't understand everything about marketing or finance or doing deals. A lot of entrepreneurs want to stay at that level—it's a sweet spot—where they're really lucrative and they're selling everything they can make and they've got a good brewpub operation going."

Kurt was quick to point out that one of the reasons they made good decisions during this period was Ann. She was not just a consigliere to Kurt, but an employee of the brewery and a part of the senior leadership. She wasn't there every day—her job as a professor came first—but she provided invaluable advice during this period of transition. "Rob and I would look at things and think, 'God, this is kind of complex.' She'd look at it and say, 'Well, this is what I would do.' She'd cut right through things that we were overly complicating. She would just cut right through and say, 'Here's what you might consider.' It was invariably wise and helpful."

The 1990s were treacherous for breweries trying to make similar leaps. They become fundamentally different businesses. Selling beer is harder and more expensive the farther away from the brewery it is. Competing regionally requires partnerships with a network of wholesalers in distant regions or states, and it means entering markets unfamiliar with the product. It requires a more engaged sales force as well as sophisticated branding and marketing. Such a transition changes company culture and operations. Present-day Kurt should cut his '90s self some slack; that leap was dangerous enough that dozens of breweries didn't make it. Caution was warranted.

The Emotional Toll of Growth

Rob and Kurt were stoic when I spoke to them about this period. Their wives, however, were able to express how challenging this time was. Barb Widmer, Rob's wife, told me, "It was hard not having their fingers in everything and not knowing everything that was going on." She described how the two founders felt such a sense of responsibility that they would stop to pick up a scrap of litter in the parking lot. Hiring someone to help with management would mean ceding some of that responsibility. That was the point, the goal, and yet they couldn't help feeling ambivalent about it. "But then they didn't know what it was like to have a manager. He wasn't going to make sure the parking lot got cleaned every day. That wasn't why he was there, but that was what *they* did!"

Ann watched the toll it took on her husband and saw much the same thing. "I think Kurt handled the stress well, but it would be wrong to say there wasn't stress. As you get more and more involved in deal-making and the financial world and a lot of personnel issues—he internalized a lot of that stress."

They understood the gravity of making the decision to grow, too. Barb continued: "Everything was flush and they'd pretty much paid things off and things were good, but somebody else had hefeweizen now in the market. It was go forward or go backward. I just know that every time they went forward with a new expansion or a new bottling line, it was like, 'Let's try this. Oh my god—how are we going to make this payment?' Every move forward came with a ton of angst."

Even around the brewery, things changed. Barb continued, "Kurt and Rob, when they first started, all these people were their coworkers. And then as they [grew], they had to be in the management position, all of a sudden they lost their friend base."

Angel Marquez, one of the first employees hired by Widmer Brothers, acknowledged that change, too. "At the beginning it felt like a real family business. Kurt and Rob are rare—they're there every day. You know it's a family business. They're always there, they're always working." Growth brought change, and as the company expanded, it necessarily became less tight-knit and more diffused. All of that weighed on the brothers.

Nevertheless, by 1994, they had decided to move forward with the intention of growing. They began by looking for someone who could step in and help with the management side of the business. By all accounts, this was the realm Rob and especially Kurt most wanted to off-load. Neither had any experience overseeing a large organization, and they wanted to bring in someone who did. They found Terry Michaelson, who had most recently been president of Etcetera Inc., a fashion retail company. Etcetera had been sold in 1993, and Michaelson was looking for a new opportunity. At that point in his career, he had the choice to move up to larger corporations—he had an offer from Disney—but he was intrigued by the chance to build a small company instead.

"I loved beer, but I didn't know anything about the industry," Michaelson said. "From Kurt and Rob's standpoint, that wasn't really important to them because they had the beer part. What they were struggling with, and didn't quite frankly want to deal with that much, was the processes and organizational structures, and what you have to do on the business side to allow the beer side to grow."

Ann Widmer sat in on the interviews, and she saw what an asset Michaelson could be to the company. "She told us, 'This guy Terry has good chemistry; he seems to just fit with who you and Rob are,'" Kurt recalled. "He's very dedicated, very conscientious, very hard-working, very earnest. His experience is something that we were lacking." Ann's support of Michaelson led to one of the best decisions Kurt recalled making.

When Michaelson arrived as the incoming CEO at the new building on Russell, the offices weren't completed yet, so he spent the first three months in a small desk packed in next to Rob and Kurt. This allowed him to absorb the particularities of the new business and get up to speed on what running a brewery entailed while watching and listening as the brothers went about their day. "It was an amazing period," he recalled.

What he took away from that experience was a series of questions, which sent him farther outside the offices. Pastore remembers his approach. "So [Terry] started to ask, 'How much beer can you make?' He asked the sales guy, 'How much beer are you selling?' Then he started visiting some of our larger customers." This led to a broader analysis of market trends, trends in consumer goods, and projections about sales growth. For the first time, the brewery was looking out three, five, and ten years, and beginning to form a plan for how to meet the expected changes on the horizon.

Shortly after they hired Michaelson, the Widmers brought in Tim McFall to do marketing. McFall had a background in branding and marketing, and he looked at Widmer's position in the market and considered how to solidify the company's image. Once again, McFall was able to bring focus and attention to subjects that had previously evolved organically.

Growing Pains

One of the brewery's early missteps garnered a period of unwanted bad press. In the early 1990s, the company's lawyers directed Kurt and Rob to ask employees to sign noncompete agreements. When one of their employees left to start his own brewery in 1993, Widmer Brothers sued him. The brewer was Alan Sprints, who would go on to found Hair of the Dog in Southeast Portland. The optics of the situation were terrible for the Widmers. As Widmer had grown, it had sought to maintain the image of a supportive local craft brewery, but local reporters painted it as a corporate giant more interested in protecting the bottom line than former employees.

Sprints recalls the events without malice. "In my mind, the noncompete agreement was to protect them. If I was to take a recipe or graphics, or do something they did, they'd be able to enforce their noncompete. Afterwards I learned that if you have a noncompete you have to enforce it 100 percent of the time, or you can't enforce it at all. So they almost had to sue me if they wanted to keep enforcing it. They didn't really have much of a leg to stand on. In the end we settled and I agreed not to make hefeweizen. It wasn't that long after the incident was over that they brought us a fruit basket and said they were sorry things worked out that way." He paused and added, "Nowadays we're on speaking terms," and laughed.

One example is illustrative. It was about this time that the brewery changed its name from Widmer to Widmer Brothers, a decision that emerged from a methodical consideration of the brand. McFall described the process: "From a marketing standpoint, one of the things that happened at about that time was a slight rebrand within the company to Widmer Brothers Brewing Company. That was deliberate, and the motivation was, if you launch a beer outside your comfort zone and you send it down to California or Texas, a lot of people don't know what Widmer is. Is it a family name? As soon as you put *Brothers* on there, people know, 'Oh, it's a couple guys who make this.' That gives it a bit of warmth."

This period of reexamination coincided with two other events. Widmer's success with Hefeweizen had not only created an entire category, but had also begun to attract serious competitors. Pyramid introduced their hefeweizen in bottles, and soon Nor'Wester would launch entirely as a hefeweizen house, also in bottles. In Portland, Michaelson and the Widmers worried that they might start losing ground if people couldn't get their Hefeweizen in bottles.

At the same time, Widmer started fielding offers from national breweries, including an offer from Miller so large that Michaelson described it as "ridiculous." These breweries hadn't found traction with their own in-house craft brands and were looking to buy into the industry; Anheuser-Busch had recently made a minority investment in Redhook, and there was a sense that more was to come. Few breweries had as many upsides as the Widmers—a flagship brand that was right in the center of the American palate and had complete dominance in the most competitive region in the country—or a product that seemed as poised to go national.

Based on these developments and Michaelson's analyses, the brewery concluded three things. Pastore summarized: "First was that the potential for the product was just amazing, and second, that we needed to get it in bottles, and third, that we were very close to capacity. So he immediately started to say, 'How do we make more beer here?'"

Widmer had just celebrated its ten-year anniversary, and they were setting the pace for success as a craft brewery. In fact, as Kurt said (in one of his rare moments of evident pride), "We were the second-largest draft-only brewery in the world. We sold 68,000 barrels in draft the last year we were draft-only." Even as recently as 2015, that would have put them among the fifty largest craft breweries in the country.

Other competitors had already introduced bottled hefeweizen. The brewery was at a familiar place again—maxed out on capacity—but this time their circumstances were even more precarious. To avoid being an also-ran in the segment they created, Widmer Brothers needed to expand again, and this time make the leap to a large, industrial-scale brewhouse.

The company was enormously profitable, but they had just completed the renovation of two historic buildings and the installation of a new brewhouse. The kind of brewery they envisioned would require a multimillion-dollar bankroll, which was beyond their means. So around 1995, the brewery started looking at ways to secure the finances to fund such an expansion. They spoke to banks and private equity, and started to seriously consider Miller's offer. And then they got a call from St. Louis.

THE PARTNERSHIP

IN OCTOBER 1997, WIDMER BROTHERS BREWERY (AS IT had been re-christened) announced that it had sold a minority share of the company to Anheuser-Busch. The country's largest brewery—then producing one of every two beers sold in the United States—would get 27 percent of Widmer and representation on the company's board. Widmer Brothers would get some cash and access to A-B's nationwide network of distributors, universally agreed to be the best in the business. There is no doubt that, aside from the release of Weizen in 1985, this was the most consequential decision Kurt and Rob ever made.

It transformed the business, allowing it to grow from a regional, all-draft brewery to a widely distributed bottled brand. In one stroke, Widmer Brothers had access to markets that would allow it to become one of the largest breweries in the United States, a worthy rival and ultimate heir to Blitz-Weinhard's status as Portland's city brewery. But equally, in the decade that followed, it became the defining fact used to assess the brewery. As craft brewing matured and grew, it was as if the brewery had an asterisk affixed to its name. Every new release, company initiative, and rebrand seemed to be evaluated with a proviso attached to it: "partly owned by Anheuser-Busch." In a world in which "small" and "independent" became watchwords for quality, anyone associated with large, multinational breweries was marked by a certain stigma.

Now, more than two decades after the partnership, many have rendered their own judgment. The Brewers Association, a trade organization for small breweries of which Widmer had long been a charter member, excommunicated them in 2007. Competitors and friends, beer geeks and journalists—many criticized the brewery for selling out or conspiring with the enemy. Sure, the partnership allowed the brewery to grow, but many people outside of the brewery felt Rob and Kurt should never have gone into business with August Busch III. Yet within the brewery, there was never much doubt. It was considered a stroke of luck that Anheuser-Busch was a willing partner, and there has been little reconsideration of the deal.

This dichotomy is instructive. While the world learned of the deal in one brief press release, the burgeoning partnership actually unfolded over many months within the brewery. Optics aside, the brewery's circumstances at the time, the benefits of the deal to Widmer Brothers, and the changing fortunes of craft beer together convinced company leaders this was an excellent opportunity. In retrospect, reasonable people may disagree about its wisdom, but in assembling the various moving parts,

Kurt and Rob at the Russell Street brewery.

it's easy enough to see why the company formed this partnership—and why most in the brewery still consider it a smart decision.

By 1993, the thirty-barrel brewhouse at Russell Street was already approaching maximum production, and Kurt and Rob were mulling the idea of another expansion. Discussions inside the brewery continued for months, and a number of factors reshaped their thinking. Perhaps foremost among them was a growing sense of confidence and ambition. It was, as always, refracted through the owners' self-deprecating, aw-shucks personalities, but it was there. Rob came the closest to voicing their aims baldly when he said, "Part of it was—maybe we had a good sleep that night—but we felt that if anyone's going to take this style national it's going to be us. We wanted to keep growing."

Kurt's wife, Ann, had as much experience observing the brothers as anyone, and she pointed it out, too. "Kurt and Rob are reserved, but they're powerful. They are really very steadfast in their belief and their passions." Few breweries were more successful at this point in American craft brewing, and Widmer's success had spawned many imitators. The national landscape was still forming, and only a few brands had managed to extend national or near-national distribution. Given the buzz surrounding Hefeweizen, there was no reason to think Widmer Brothers couldn't join that select group.

At earlier moments in the business, Rob and Kurt had to make decisions based on incomplete information or were so consumed with making beer that they didn't have time for lengthy strategic planning. This moment was different in its magnitude, and it called for more deliberation—and with a newly expanded leadership team, they could afford to do it. When the leadership team stopped to consider their options, they discovered that risks awaited no matter which direction they turned.

They stood at one of those decisive crossroads in a company's evolution. In the ostensibly safer choice, a company proceeds along a path of slow growth, focusing on a local or regional strategy and keeping its debt low. This sacrifices certain options for rapid growth but minimizes the chance of failure. In the riskier course, the company takes on debt to finance a large capital expansion with the goal of reaching a much larger audience.

As they explored both paths, the brothers unearthed several hazards of staying on the supposedly safe path. Rob pointed out that if it didn't continue to grow, the brewery would risk losing its most talented people to breweries that offered more opportunities. Also worrisome was the increasingly fierce competition in the wheat beer category; if they failed to grow, they'd be in a weaker position to fend off challengers.

There was a structural problem, as well. Because it was still a draft-only brewery, Widmer Brothers couldn't compete in the segment where most of the beer was sold: at the supermarket. Already maxed out with the thirty-barrel brewery, Widmer Brothers didn't have the capacity to expand into bottles while still making enough beer to meet its draft orders.

"You have to remember that bottles—packaged product—were still 80 percent of the market," Kurt said. "And we weren't able to participate in any of that. So to be significant to our wholesalers, we needed to have bottles to participate in that segment, too." Growth meant taking on more debt and more obvious, direct risk, but failing to grow was fraught with danger as well.

A pivotal meeting came in 1994 when all the stakeholders gathered to discuss the future. Everyone at that meeting agreed: instead of another small step, the brewery should take a leap into the future. "We had the meeting," Rob said. "Hefe was draft-only and was still blowing up, but a couple of our competitors were nipping at us. Jim Bernau of Nor'Wester had just come out and said, 'I'm going to brew Widmer Hefe and put it in a bottle.' We talked about letting that brewery over there define how big we got, but everybody in that room was frozen in their position at that point. We all agreed to get bigger."

Deciding to grow resolved two immediate, interlocking issues. First, Widmer would design and build a new, purpose-built brewery to make Hefeweizen. It would instantly give the brewery an upper capacity of 250,000 barrels, eight times the size of their current capacity. Second, they would fill that capacity by moving into bottled beer. But with every answer, more questions arose, and for Widmer Brothers, two came to the front of the line. Where would they get the money to expand, and how would they push the beer farther out into the country?

The Big New Brewery

If you wanted a large brewery in 1995, you didn't just start Googling. And you couldn't call the manufacturer down the road; all the large brewery fabricators were located in Europe. It may seem that, for a company that had already built three breweries, expanding to a fourth would be intuitive enough. But in a very real way, it was like starting from scratch. Transitioning from a thirty-barrel brewhouse to a 250-barrel system is like trading in a bicycle for a new pickup. Everything is different: the way the system is automated, the design and function of the vessels, and the way it integrates all elements of the process, from the grain silo to the packaging floor. The Widmers would be leaving behind their direct-fire brewhouse and moving to a new steam system, going from a hands-on process to an automated one. And because none of the information was readily available, someone had to figure it all out. Rather than handle it themselves, Kurt and Rob made the surprising decision to give the task to Sebastian Pastore. He describes the process below:

"I remember being twenty-seven and volunteering to Kurt to research brewhouse manufacturers. I went to the *Modern Brewer* magazine and looked in the back. It was pre-internet then, '94, '95. I remember typing up letters on WordPerfect and printing them out one at a time on Widmer stationery and faxing them to brewhouse manufacturers.

"At some point there were several buildings across the street from us; they were sort of clustered together. Everybody's talking about how we need to expand and where are we going to go. Terry and I are having some conversations and trying to figure out—we were very, very inexperienced—but how do you do site location? Should we put this on Swan Island? Truck traffic, logistics, all that kind of stuff. And then Kurt comes back across the street into the front door of the brewery one day and just announces to Terry that he and Rob have bought the building across the street, and that's where we're going to build the brewery. Terry and I looked at each other, and we laugh about that to this day. We were like, 'Ooooh-*kay*! I guess that's what we're going to do.'

"So I'm faxing away to Europe for brewhouse quotes and beginning to talk to the architect about doing conceptual designs for the brewery on that space—what do we tear down? What do we remodel? We had an architect that we were working with whose office was and still is right up the street named Mark Garvey, who had worked with Kurt on the renovation of the original Smithson and McKay block. We were designing it as we went. In the middle of the project, we decided we needed to add a packaging facility. Well. We started out building the front seat and along the way we added the car.

"I had engaged three manufacturers by fax. Briggs, which was an English manufacturer, had just built a brewery for Shiner. And then Huppmann and Ziemann from Germany. So I proceed to get quotes, do research, figure out how big it is, how many vessels, what do we want? Does it include fermentation, all the rest of that. At a certain point, Kurt and Rob—it was mostly Rob, the Jiminy Cricket conscience of the beer—kept asking, 'How are you going to do this and how are you going to guarantee us that the beer is going to be exactly the same?' It was a big, big question. There was literally no way to deliver that guarantee, and at a certain point you had to take some things on faith. There are 100,000 breweries in the world and they've all figured out how to do this; we're going to figure it out as well.

"One of the things that was interesting in the context of our talking to Huppmann, and later, Anheuser-Busch, is that when there's an incredible difference in, just orders of magnitude difference in, experience and technical expertise and size and scale, the relationship is different than it is between two peers. So I would go to Huppmann and say, 'I'm really worried that our steam-fired brewing system won't produce exactly the same Hefeweizen as our thirty-five-barrel JV Northwest system.' And they would say with their German arrogance, 'Pish posh; this is the way we do it. You should just buy a Huppmann brew-house and the beer will always be very, very good.'

"I ended up flying around the world on sponsored visits with each of these outfits. Went to a couple breweries in England for Briggs, and then to Germany to see Ziemann and Huppmann brewhouses. It gets down to the wire and I think Huppmann's the right one, and I'm talking to Al Triplett, the VP of brewing at Redhook—he had one Huppmann brewhouse running and another one in process. I went up and visited him several times and looked at what he'd done. They were using one in Chico, and I'd been down to see Ken Grossman and his new Huppmann brewhouse. So we eventually decided on Huppmann."

WHY WIDMER BROTHERS CHOSE ANHEUSER-BUSCH

By the early 1990s, both Wall Street and the larger national breweries had begun to take note of craft brewing. When they were trying to get started a decade earlier, banks roundly laughed in Kurt and Rob's faces. Now that they had demonstrated the public's thirst for their beer, they had many suitors. Long before they entered discussions with Anheuser-Busch, they found funding to launch their expansions. "We originally got some private equity along with debt, and that was how we arranged the first financing," CEO Terry Michaelson explained. That allowed Widmer to proceed with the new brewhouse right away.

As they went through the long process of finding land for their new facility, designing a building, and installing a 250-barrel brewhouse, other suitors came knocking. Around 1994, the big national breweries "all came to town," Kurt recalled. "Except Coors. Everyone except Coors," he said, laughing. They formed a procession, but this was the early days of craft, and not all made a convincing case. "The guys who owned Heileman at that point—a firm out of Texas—they might have been the first. It was an insulting meeting. They just played us as chumps from the stumps and basically offered us a ridiculous price. I mean, we were unsophisticated, not that smart, but we were smart enough to see that these guys were ridiculous." The really big offer came from Miller—then still an independent brewery—which wanted to buy them outright.

At that point, Widmer Brothers wasn't looking for a partner and didn't absolutely need one. Their arrangement with the private equity firm Desai Capital Management allowed them to move forward on their plans. They had covered almost all the challenges they could see on the horizon. "We identified five components that we needed to have," Kurt said. "We needed to have the best people, which we did; we needed to have state-of-the-art brewing, which we did; we needed to have a solid financial footing; we needed to have excellent beer; and we needed to have access to market. And the only thing we couldn't control was access to market."

That last point was critical, and it made the offer of one final brewery very appealing. Anheuser-Busch had recently completed a partnership with Redhook Brewery in Seattle. In that arrangement, A-B took a minority stake in Redhook and seats on their board, and in exchange gave Redhook access to their distribution system. It was a novel approach—particularly when viewed from our current moment, when AB InBev just buys breweries outright—but one in which both parties saw large advantages.

Paul Shipman, Redhook founder and then-CEO, relayed the way he viewed his situation right before striking his own deal. "I didn't have an elaborate, well-thought-out distribution strategy. So I decided to focus on that and figure out if there was a better way to do it. Wherever you went in the United States in those days, there were three or four distributors that you'd want to do business with. There would be the Bud guys, the Miller guys, and the Coors guys. What we knew in the Pacific Northwest was that we liked the Bud guys. They paid their bills, they had the market share, they were good to work with. So I thought, 'I want to be with the Budweiser guys, and I'd like to do that coast to coast.'" For Shipman, that coast-to-coast arrangement made all the sense in the world. By partnering with Anheuser-Busch, he immediately had access to markets anywhere in the country.

This was what attracted Widmer Brothers as well. Of those five objectives they'd identified, working with A-B would give them the final piece: access to markets. In one stroke of the pen, the brewery would effectively ink relationships with distributors in every corner of the country. Because of the Redhook deal, there was already an appealing blueprint in place, which made the whole partnership even more enticing. Widmer Brothers didn't have to guess how it would work if they joined A-B—they had a case study in what would happen.

In addition to distribution, Widmer Brothers received $18 million, another attractive inducement. Still, there was one final, unexpected sweetener in the deal: the Widmers and Anheuser-Busch CEO August Busch III really hit it off. This is one of the most surprising elements of the entire Widmer story. If you imagined that the house of Widmer would ally only uneasily with the famous Busch family of St. Louis, you'd guess wrong. Kurt in particular had a meeting of the minds with Busch.

"For years, Kurt had a picture of himself with August on the wall," Sebastian Pastore said. "He really resonated with Kurt. A lot of August's values were Kurt's values."

Ann Widmer offered an example. "[Busch] walked through the brewery and said things like, 'First clean [micro] brewery I've ever been in.' He wanted to be able to eat off the floor, and that's what we presented to him. There was that mutual admiration; Kurt said, 'Yes! Finally, someone who gets it.' He was a brewer who believed in those same extreme standards of conscientiousness and cleanliness and everything. It wasn't just on paper; he liked August."

The feeling, by all accounts, was mutual. Tony Short, Director of Business and Wholesaler Involvement for Anheuser-Busch at the time, and an executive who was involved in the deal, saw it too. "He thought it was a very well-made product, and August Busch was a stickler for quality. It was at the heart of everything he did. He liked Kurt." While in discussions about the Widmer deal, Short gave a presentation to an internal strategy committee, and he had help from a powerful ally. "As I was about to begin the presentation, August III jumped in and gave a three-minute intro about what great people they were, how solid the beers were and everything. That made the presentation go a lot smoother."

As I interviewed people who had worked in the brewery during this era, many told "August stories." He was a vivid personality whose commitment to running a tight ship often bordered on the comic. Kurt relayed a story he'd heard from one of the brewmasters at an A-B facility. "'When he's on an inspection, we'll leave a piece of sandwich in the fridge or something like that for him to find because he won't stop until he finds something.' A number of people told us that—'We'll leave a red herring because he won't stop until he finds something.'"

Pastore told one story about how Busch, upon hearing that the bottling line was down, immediately charged out of their meeting to race to the packaging floor. He continued, "A classic August Busch story is he's flying to one of his breweries on his plane and he saw that the guy who was cutting the big green lawn in front of the brewery—you know how a lawnmower will leave a darker stripe and a lighter stripe? Well, apparently August didn't like the way they were lined up, so he got off the plane and stormed in and [told him how to do it properly]. There are many, many stories like that."

I had a chance to speak with August Busch III, and he confirmed the tight relationship with the Widmers. "They're true gentlemen. They're the kind of family and operation that you don't have to have a bunch of paper and sign things; you can shake hands, look a person in the eye, and know that a deal's a deal. That's the kind of people they are."

From the Widmers' perspective, it all aligned. Leaving aside the respect August Busch III and the Widmers shared, it made obvious sense on paper. But Terry Michaelson mentioned something that had already become a theme for these brothers, and would remain so throughout their lives. "Before we made the decision with Anheuser-Busch, I brought in a number of people for Kurt and Rob to listen to," he explained. "Part of what I was talking to them about was, 'Listen, the amount of money that Miller is offering you is ridiculous, and you can't think that this will always come along. There's *lots* of upside.'"

Their response was characteristic of their whole approach. When given a question about business and money, they always came up with an answer about beer. Terry continued: "For them, it really was, 'Hey, we're having fun making beer, and at the end of the day if we end up leaving millions on the table, we're fine with that as long as the journey's interesting and we're making great beer.'" They did the A-B deal because it made the most sense from a brewing perspective.

WHY ANHEUSER-BUSCH CHOSE WIDMER BROTHERS

In St. Louis, executives at Anheuser-Busch began to take note of "microbreweries" in the early 1990s. Their thinking as this deal evolved—along with the Redhook partnership—is not directly germane to the Widmer story. The team in Portland knew what they were getting into when they joined Anheuser-Busch. But in the larger sense—the state of beer at the time, how it evolved, and the linkages and discontinuities between "big beer" and "craft"—it is critical if you want to understand the way beer has evolved in the United States in the past forty years.

Two people sat ringside during this period and were closely involved in guiding the process. Tony Short was an executive during this period and sat in on the key meetings as the discussions unfolded. Mitch Steele came from the craft world and knew Rob and Kurt from his days working at a brewpub in California. He would later be hired as Stone Brewing's brewmaster, but at the time he was doing new product development at A-B in St. Louis.

Anheuser-Busch's first response to the micro trend of the late 1980s was entirely predictable—they tried to co-opt it. "I got involved in this because we were trying to do our own kind of craft brand at the time," Steele said. The trouble was, they weren't selling. It was early enough in the era that no one was entirely sure why any of the craft brands were succeeding. Steele continued to experiment, thinking that the challenge might have been finding the right beer for the market. "Some of them were really good beers," he said. "Some of them were just amped up Budweiser lagers, but some of them were really quite good." Part of it, he acknowledged, was because the sales and marketing team didn't know how to handle niche beers—but this wasn't the central problem.

To figure out what was going on, Anheuser-Busch commissioned a study and made an important discovery. Tony Short explained: "At the time, the market research that Anheuser-Busch was doing indicated that consumers viewed craft-like offerings from big brewers differently than they viewed craft products produced by small breweries." It wasn't so much that the beer wasn't "craft"—it's that Anheuser-Busch wasn't. Short's conclusion? If they didn't partner with actual craft breweries, they were "going to be shut out of the segment."

Understanding Distribution

So much of the story about the Widmer Brothers/ Anheuser-Busch partnership comes back to distribution. Getting a pint or bottle of beer from the brewery to the consumer's hand is a far more complicated, circuitous process than most people realize. When a brewery is small and selling in a single local market, matters are simple enough. But once the beer has to travel any distance, and particularly when it crosses state lines, a brewery has to figure out how to get their beer to those distant grocery stores, restaurants, and pubs while it is still fresh and tasty.

For national brands, setting up distribution networks is critical to reaching the market. Wholesalers become the face of the brewery in those distant locations. The level and quality of service, the responsiveness, and the expertise they provide either helps or hinders the brewery's entrance into that market. The business works in the other direction, too. For a wholesaler, the portfolio of beers they can offer to those retailers is critical for their own competitiveness. The tricky part? Once a brewery and distributor agree to work together in a particular location, the deal has no expiration date and is very difficult for either party to exit. Neither a wholesaler nor a brewery will enter into this partnership lightly.

This is why many people familiar with the A-B/ Widmer deal viewed it largely as a distribution deal. Both parties received enormous benefits. Anheuser-Busch's distributors were widely regarded as the best in the business, and Widmer Brothers got immediate access to them without the headache of negotiating with each company one by one. A national network alone wasn't adequate; the individual wholesalers had to be excellent. Finally, it was a "clean" arrangement: when Widmer Brothers came on board, the A-B wholesalers didn't carry other craft brands that Widmer would have had to compete with.

The wholesalers, which in many cases were hungering for craft brands in their portfolios, finally had something to offer retailers. Anheuser-Busch picked up valued brands instantly, without having to build them up. Additionally, they received a fee for acting as the distributor and were able to lock these brands down nationally. There were certainly other benefits for both companies, but their interlocking needs found their solution through Anheuser-Busch's national network of wholesalers.

Both Steele and Short thought they needed to compete in the craft segment. Steele, the once and future craft brewer, expected it to grow, and Short felt it was important that A-B compete in absolutely every niche to avoid falling behind in trending segments. However, that was not a universal view. Within the company, "there was the contingent that thought it was a joke," Steele explained. "They looked at it and said, 'These guys don't know what the hell they're doing. They don't know anything about brewing and they're brewing these beers that taste like smoke and electrical fires and hop resin. What the hell are they doing?'"

Nationally speaking, little guys and their electrical fires wouldn't have been a problem worth sweating—the numbers then were still tiny, particularly for a company selling over a hundred million barrels of beer—except for one thing: wholesalers. Anheuser-Busch had just initiated a program called 100 Percent Share of Mind to encourage its wholesalers to carry only A-B products. It was controversial because competitors in both the brewing and wholesaling tiers assumed it would restrict competition. And they weren't wrong. That's the conclusion August Busch III came to when he introduced the program: "Each of you [must] exert your undivided attention and total efforts on Anheuser-Busch products. If you sell our competitors' products, can you still give us your best efforts? I don't think so."

Craft wasn't a big deal nationally, but it had become significant in certain cities. That put A-B's wholesalers in those jurisdictions in a bind. "Real craft brewers that were being carried by Budweiser distributors were selling," Steel explained. But there was a problem. "If we—Anheuser-Busch—were going to require our wholesalers to be 100 percent exclusive, we [had] to give them some offerings that made them competitive. That's where this whole thing started." Partnering with Redhook and Widmer would give A-B craft choices to offer wholesalers.

Before inking the deal with Anheuser-Busch, Widmer Brothers signed on with wholesaler Maletis Beverage in

Portland. This was part of their plan to add bottles to their portfolio, but it was convenient that Maletis was a local A-B distributor. Rob Maletis, the third-generation owner of the company, used a modern example to explain the situation A-B confronted as craft beer claimed larger and larger percentages in certain cities (especially Portland, where craft was more popular than in any other city).

The same thing happened with Heineken just recently, he said. "Heineken's got a network of distributors that are loyal to them, and [they're thinking], 'Should we get something in our portfolio to take advantage of this high-end business?' Clearly, someone like Heineken doesn't even have one share here. There's no doubt that if you're at Heineken and you're looking at a major metro market that's craft-centric like Seattle and Portland, you're going, 'What happened to my business?'" That was what led the Dutch giant to purchase Lagunitas in 2015—and what sent A-B looking for craft partners back in the 1990s.

Another question nagged at Short during the negotiations: what if craft brewing became a significant portion of the market? He saw significant upside to investing in craft, and risk in failing to do so. "What I would always tell people at Anheuser-Busch [was] to consider this an insurance policy," he said. "If the craft segment dies out, we made these small investments and had very little headache, and in the meantime, we've brought to our wholesalers a product that we cannot by definition bring them. They're our partners, they're largely exclusive, and we owe our wholesaler family products in every segment in order to compete. So it was a win-win-win. For very little risk, we were able to check a lot of boxes."

So far, all of this makes sense. But why didn't Anheuser-Busch just buy Widmer outright, as Miller, Heileman, and others offered to do? Eventually, Anheuser-Busch InBev would make that choice, but at the time they worried it would backfire. Their reasoning goes back to that market research about which beer customers were willing to buy, and A-B's failure to sell their own brands.

"Remember the problem we were trying to solve for," Short said. "At the time, what we believed was that we had this situation where the consumer viewed products from large breweries differently than they viewed them from craft brewers. By taking minority stakes we were able to effectively claim—and it was true, of course—that, look: We're not running the company. These are still true craft brewers, and all of the romance and consumer perception and benefit that comes with being small craft was maintained. If we buy a majority of the company, then those consumers are going to look at them as though they sold out—they're big beer now. That was the cornerstone of the strategy; it was anchored in that belief."

At the end of the day, it was an easy call for Anheuser-Busch to make. For minimal cost, they were able to enter the craft segment, and deals with Redhook and Widmer Brothers gave their wholesalers broader choices. Some within the brewery assumed the fad would die, and this was a low-cost, low-risk method of participating while it was hot. It didn't hurt that August Busch III—the president, CEO, and board chair—liked Kurt and Rob

Widmer and admired their brewery. It may seem like an odd arrangement now, but at the time A-B believed taking a minority stake was the only way their investment would hold its value.

THE EFFECT OF THE PARTNERSHIP

It was touch-and-go for a few months. Talks for the deal stretched on long enough that, by the time it was finally completed, craft beer had entered the first serious market correction. Angel Marquez, who was working in the brewhouse at the time, remembers doing a lot of cleaning in those first months, waiting for the orders to roll in and get the big new mash tun humming. "As soon as they get it going, after they've got it staffed up to do all this production, the whole market falls flat," he said.

This coincided with the move into bottles. For years, Widmer had been reluctant to bottle because they didn't want Hefeweizen's iconic haze to settle out. (Because of these challenges, Barb Widmer recalls Rob telling her, "We are *never* gonna bottle!" when she met him in 1992.) They eventually figured it out, and the new brewery was designed to optimize bottling Hefeweizen so it could be sent far from Oregon and still arrive in its characteristic cloudy form.

Crafting a New Bottle

In 2001, Widmer Brothers introduced a striking new bottle. In a time when nearly every brewery bought generic bottles in bulk, the Widmer bottles featured the brewery's "W" inset in the neck. It gave them distinctiveness and elegance, which served as a visual metaphor for the Widmer approach. Tim McFall, the marketing director during the project, described how the bottle came to be:

"We were looking at the proliferation of craft beer at the time and, not all of them, but the vast majority, were in the standard, stock bottle—we'll call it the Sierra Nevada bottle. Our biggest competitor in the Northwest was Pyramid, and they were using that bottle. As we looked to launch into new marketplaces and separate ourselves from the masses, we thought we needed to have a better-looking bottle; we needed a more premium-looking bottle.

"One of the things that was happening at the time was, with proliferating products came price discounting. There was a lot of competition out there that was just flooding the marketplace. So we took a different tack. We thought, instead of lowering our price, let's increase our value. The research we did at the time was showcasing the standard Widmer bottle versus the longneck, and the longneck was [perceived to be] worth more. We moved into the longneck bottle to give us the insurance of not having to discount as much as our competition.

"Somewhere along the line we decided to go to a custom bottle. That was not an easy discussion, because the bottle *did* become more expensive. That was kind of hard for us to swallow as we were launching into new markets. All of a sudden our margins get tighter because the bottle's more expensive. When you're looking at a couple million bottles, even if it's a penny a bottle, it's a huge impact at the end of the year.

"We had to change the bottling line to accommodate the different bottles, and we had to completely change all of our packaging. So that was a big step for the company. But, whether you're in brewing or in the cellar or a sales guy, marketing guy—everybody took tremendous pride in everything that was being done. So when we launched a new bottle, everybody thought it was very cool because it was *ours*."

In the end, there is no doubt that this partnership helped cement Widmer Brothers as one of the nation's biggest breweries. Once the deal was done, Widmer Brothers beer went out on trucks across 18 states. It got East Coast distribution and even made an appearance on *Seinfeld* in the late 1990s. The new brewhouse allowed Widmer Brothers to produce the highest-quality beer it had ever made. A new, state-of-the-art lab helped monitor the beer and assure consistency as it traveled the country. Even with the downturn in the market, these moves allowed the brewery to prosper. "We actually had a better growth pattern than most people," CEO Terry Michaelson said. "It just wasn't as dramatic. I don't think we ever had a year where we were negative in sales."

The partnership produced other benefits the brewery hadn't foreseen. "That's been a critical piece of our success, and it's paid off in ways we didn't even anticipate," Kurt said.

Kurt inspecting the very first bottling run, c. 1994.

"We'd ask [Anheuser-Busch] things like, 'Can we piggyback on you for purchasing glass, hops, malt?' They were like, 'Let's see now, it won't cost us anything—why *wouldn't* we do that?' But that wasn't envisioned when we started."

On the other hand, some of the benefits they forecast were overly optimistic. Terry Michaelson had a front-row seat to the unexpected challenges that cropped up. "We maybe underestimated how many resources we were going to have to put into the market," he said. "The thing in retrospect that we didn't understand was how hard it was going to be for beers—the brand—to travel outside the region. I know there are many brands that are trying to do it now, but it's really, really hard."

They also failed to take into account some basic costs. "There were questions that we didn't ask," Michaelson continued. "Like what was the total impact on your margin when you were shipping beers across the country? I mean, people knew it was going to cost more, but your margins were great and it was incremental and you had higher utilization so you didn't really think about it that much."

Despite these challenges, the logistics and implementation of the arrangement were, on balance, far more positive than negative. Going back to that initial calculus in choosing between two paths, growth or stasis, no choice was without its drawbacks. Given the late-'90s downturn—one that put 8 percent of American breweries out of business—it was especially beneficial. The scattered difficulties Widmer Brothers encountered were nothing the company wasn't prepared to deal with. Well, perhaps with one big exception.

BLOWBACK

After the announcement that Anheuser-Busch would be taking a minority stake in the brewery, perception of Widmer Brothers changed. In the classic origin myth, craft brewers existed as a reaction against the dehumanizing scale of industrial breweries. Craft brewers portrayed themselves as artisans who cared more about their sumptuous elixirs than the bottom line; they threatened to upset the dominant order of mass-market beer, but were themselves threatened by the might of the industrial giants. They were spunky little dissidents. This narrative took on the contours of a moral struggle. And so, when the Widmers threw in with Anheuser-Busch, many of their customers felt like they'd been betrayed.

To be clear, the majority of Widmer's consumers were either unaware of the partnership or didn't care. But to some of the people closest to the brewery—their most ardent fans, people within the local brewing community, their own and partners' staffs—it didn't sit right.

This sense of betrayal was something Rob and Kurt understood and even sympathized with. "You know, I remember taking shots at [A-B]," Rob said. "They were a nameless, faceless corporation. I think it's a quirk in our society that you can be too big for your britches and we love to see number one get shot down. It's fashionable to rail against the man and all that."

Inside the walls of the brewery, the Widmers went through a mental evolution. Over the course of years, they had come to believe that growth would enable the brewery to make better beer and allow it to travel farther from the brewery. Working with Anheuser-Busch facilitated that evolution. "I played that game until we *met* them," Rob concluded. "Once we met those guys, it was like, 'Shit, they're just like us.'"

That same slow evolution didn't happen outside the walls of the brewery. Instead, the news landed like a bomb, without warning. In Oregon, consumers had begun to grow wary of opportunism in craft brewing. To cite one example, in 1995, a mysterious product started showing up on shelves. It was purportedly made by the Oregon Ale and Beer Company—which turned out to be a contract-brewing arm of Boston Beer. The national breweries, having learned that consumers wouldn't buy craft-style beers made under their names, set up fake brands with bucolic, small-timey names to lure customers. By the mid-'90s, some micros had become relative giants themselves. All of this seemed to threaten the viability of the littlest players.

Widmer had grown so fast that it was already gathering suspicion among those wary of gigantism. With the announcement of the A-B deal, a narrative quickly solidified: Widmer was no longer the local boys done good. At best they were sellouts; at worst, Anheuser-Busch had taken full control and used Rob and Kurt as fig leaves to conceal the real power behind the brewery. Widmer's growth and success, combined with the involvement of Anheuser-Busch, reinforced this perception and kept it alive over the next two decades.

For Kurt and Rob, it was a painful situation. Kurt described his feelings about this period: "What I also remember—Rob and I agonized over this forever—was being told, 'You're too big.' That was part of the romance of craft brewing. Nobody ever says to Levi's, 'You guys are too big. You guys own the jeans market. Shame on you; I'm not buying your jeans.' Or Adidas shoes. And we were still a pimple on the brewing business, and all of a sudden we're *too big*. Nobody ever did say, 'Your beer is bad,' but they told us to our face and behind our backs, 'You guys are too big.' It was frustrating."

Rob pointed out that the very passion their critics expressed was what allowed them to prosper in the first place. "It's more of an emotional thing, so there's really no logic to their decision. You can usually try to tell them how things work, but it's just an emotional thing. On the other hand, it's good people get emotional about it. It would be worse if they were completely indifferent. Beer's really emotional to people."

To this day, most people who have heard of Widmer's deal with Anheuser-Busch think A-B took a controlling share, though time has changed the emotional valence of the situation. Since about 2015, news of a brewery sale has come every month or two. The shock of brewery sales has dimmed, as has that sense of betrayal. At the same time, Widmer Brothers has remained a steady presence in Portland. Kurt and Rob have been brewing beer in the city for over three decades, and stopping into the brewery has become a habit for many Portlanders. The brothers are visible members of the brewing community. Widmer sponsors local sports teams. With the brewery's constant presence in Portland, most drinkers no longer get caught up in the abstruse question of ownership—after a couple decades, it's hard for most people to consider Widmer Brothers anything but a local institution.

Since selling part of the company to Anheuser-Busch, Widmer Brothers has made a number of other high-profile partnerships. Redhook and Widmer entered into those early partnerships with Anheuser-Busch and would later combine to form Craft Brew Alliance. All of these decisions marked important milestones for the company. In many respects, however, they were merely downstream consequences of that decision to partner with A-B. It transformed the company and would eventually make it the country's ninth-largest brewery and the fourth-largest craft brewery.

From the beer side—which was always the dimension Kurt and Rob could see most clearly—it was judged an unambiguous success. "We knew at the same time that that our beer had gotten so much better," Kurt said. "Our people were better, our equipment was better, the distribution network was better. Our customers were getting a better glass of beer than ever." For people outside the brewery, the decision to sell a portion of the company to Anheuser-Busch will never be judged purely positive. Big breweries carry too much negative publicity in the craft world for that. But inside the brewery—even acknowledging the prevailing opinion elsewhere—there are few who look backward with much regret.

THE MODERN ERA

WHEN WE SAT DOWN TO DISCUSS HIS QUARTER century with the brewery, Sebastian Pastore described the most recent era of Widmer Brothers as a consequence of an earlier decision. He was talking about the Craft Brew Alliance era, when Widmer Brothers, Redhook, Kona, and others came together to form a collective of breweries. For Pastore, this configuration was hardly accidental; it proceeded from one of those moments when a choice sets into motion a series of events that fall like dominoes, leading to the present moment.

"When I look back on Widmer, I see it as a series of fateful decisions that resonated for decades afterward," Pastore said. By his reckoning there were three of these decisions. The first two had to do with expansion and physical siting of the brewery. "And then the Anheuser-Busch deal defined the rest of the brewery's history in a bunch of different ways," he concluded.

The Craft Brew Alliance began as a loose marketing partnership between Redhook and Widmer Brothers and has since become the tenth largest brewery in the country. This new company's headquarters is located within the brewery complex on North Russell Street and includes many of the old hands who began when all the beers coming off the bottling line said "Widmer" on them. Despite Widmer's central place in the new brewery, though, it now shares a byline with its partners, and, as of a few years ago, is no longer the bestseller among them. It is in many ways a surprising turn of events, but one that flowed from that key decision of the brewery's namesake founders.

FURTHER ALLIANCES

The decade following the partnership with Anheuser-Busch seemed to confirm the wisdom of the deal. "From 1997 until, say, the InBev deal, it was really all upside," Pastore said. "It was a great honeymoon period." The A-B partnership came right at the moment the craft segment of the beer market really slowed, and it wouldn't pick up again for several years. The enormous expansion in the early 1990s hadn't prepared many breweries for life during flat sales; most breweries just tried to stay in business, and few grew. In contrast, Widmer Brothers was far better positioned because of its ability to send beer farther from its home base in the Pacific Northwest, allowing the company to see continued growth. Two years after striking the deal, Widmer had boosted volume and was selling in eighteen states.

Michaelson described the period in similarly positive terms, but pointed out that not everything went as planned. Part of this, he explained, had to do with the increased cost of shipping beer across the country. But the thing they really didn't anticipate was how hard it was to enter new regions and try to build the brand, particularly in an era when craft beer was retrenching, not expanding. Hefeweizen basically sold itself in the Pacific Northwest, but in distant markets, nobody knew who Widmer was or what to expect from this oddly named beer. "It started to have a huge impact when you had to start dropping people in, and you had the costs in terms of how long it's going to take you to build your base of business in a market," Michaelson said.

Meanwhile, in Seattle, Anheuser-Busch's other partner had embarked on a more aggressive strategy for expansion. In 1996, Redhook made the bold decision to build a facility in New Hampshire and expand distribution to the East Coast. By 1998, it had become a national brand, with distribution in forty-eight states. It nevertheless came at a dangerous moment. Many of the bigger US craft brewers built large new breweries during this period in anticipation of future growth, as Widmer Brothers had done. But with the market slowdown, there was far less demand nationally than there was capacity in all these new breweries. Although the brewery had become one of the largest in the country, Redhook wasn't profitable. In 1998, it shut down its original Fremont brewery in Seattle, and during the early years of the new century it struggled to stay solvent. In 2007, CEO Paul Shipman told the *Seattle Times*, "We hung on at times by our fingernails."

In order to understand why it would ultimately make sense to form the brewery alliances that characterize the CBA—which may not seem obvious given the breweries' trajectories—Pastore pointed to the structural elements of the original arrangement with Anheuser-Busch. The biggest advantage of the partnership for both parties ran through A-B's national distribution network. In order to make such a system work, however, Widmer beer was added to Anheuser-Busch's product stream. It functioned, at least from where Anheuser-Busch distributors sat, like an A-B product.

"It's not too much of an exaggeration to say that Widmer only had one customer," Pastore explained. "Every single case of beer that we sold was sold to Anheuser-Busch and then resold to all of their distributors. We operated under something called a Master Distribution Agreement, whereby they were in effect a master distributor. We conducted business on a day-to-day basis like any other brewery. In the early days we took fax orders, and in later days we operated on their AOM—automated order management—system. And then every day I think we'd get a wire transfer from Anheuser-Busch and a big file that reconciled payments for all the shipments. All of our sales flowed through them and all of the money flowed back."

From Anheuser-Busch's perspective, combining the operations of these two Northwest breweries would streamline the whole process. Beginning as early as the late 1990s, A-B encouraged the two to consider a marriage. Pastore described it colorfully: "You have to remember that they were a $16 billion company and they owned a part ownership stake in two companies that were, at that time, maybe $150 million together. We were a pimple on their butt. And they had *two* pimples. Wouldn't it just be a lot simpler if we rolled these two together?"

In 2004, Widmer Brothers and Redhook did come together to form the first iteration of CBA. At that point, however, they were just combining a few of their departments. Michaelson described how the relationship began: "During that phase there were discussions with A-B that caused us to start the merger with Redhook. We first formed a company called Craft *Brands* Alliance, which was a sales and marketing [deal]." The arrangement wasn't a merger, though—just a way for the two companies to streamline their operations. Michaelson continued: "On the West Coast, the Craft Brands Alliance group sold the product. We consolidated salesforce, key account calls, wholesaler calls and all of that. We got a lot of efficiencies. From a model standpoint it made a lot of sense; we were probably ahead of things."

From there, things proceeded in increments. During this period, the current company, Craft Brew Alliance, began to take shape. The first big addition came in 2006, two years after CBA formed, when Widmer Brothers took a substantial stake in Chicago's Goose Island Beer Company. Having learned the limitations of selling beer far from their home base, Michaelson and the Widmers were trying a different approach: extending their union of breweries with strength in different regions of the country. Ann Widmer remembered the thinking at the time: "We could have a brewery on the East Coast," she said, referring to Redhook's New Hampshire facility, "a brewery on the West Coast, and now Goose Island in the middle, which would be a really good thing for distribution."

Central to this arrangement was Anheuser-Busch's wholesale network. To make the deal work, A-B contributed $12 million to buy out Goose Island's existing distributor contracts. The purchase also allowed Goose Island owner John Hall to pay off the brewery's original investors. By shifting to the A-B network, Goose Island saw an immediate bump. This was even true in the Chicago market, where A-B's wholesalers were reaching eight times as many accounts as Goose Island's old wholesalers.

It was a minor acquisition at the time and attracted minimal attention. Because Widmer Brothers were the headline buyers—not Anheuser-Busch—the deal caused very little disturbance in Chicago. It was the first step into a new model of expansion, one that extended beyond the natural affinity between Redhook and Widmer Brothers. It also served as an example for others to follow. Within a few years, a dozen or more affiliations between craft breweries would form—some among peers, others organized under larger companies like Gambrinus or Duvel Moortgat.

With Goose Island now in the CBA family, Anheuser-Busch was developing a stable of craft brands for its wholesalers. By the year of the Goose deal, craft beer had recovered from the market correction of the 1990s and was at the start of a decade-long run of double-digit growth. Mass-market lagers, by contrast, were beginning their decline, and A-B's portfolio fell 2 percent in 2005. In 2006, the craft segment constituted just 3.4 percent of the overall beer market; a decade later, it was approaching 15 percent. Meanwhile, domestic lagers began a losing streak that trimmed the market share of leading brands year after year. Anheuser-Busch recognized all of this earlier than most other large beer companies. Five years later, in 2011, the newly globalized AB InBev would embark on its own new strategy by buying Goose Island from CBA, the first step in creating their High End portfolio of craft brands.

ENTER KONA

The next piece of the future alliance happened very casually, when Widmer Brothers started contract brewing for Kona, a small brewpub on Hawaii's Big Island. This alliance hadn't started as a grand scheme, but was rather the result of a relationship between friends. Kurt had known Kona founder Cameron Healy for years, so when Kona's bottling line went down, the two discussed whether Widmer Brothers could package a batch for them. At that time, Widmer's brewery was so big that even a single batch would have been more beer than Kona could handle. When the possibility came up again a few years later, Kona had grown enough that brewing in Portland made sense. In 2001, Widmer Brothers began to brew Kona for the first time.

Because of the friendship connection between the two companies and Kona's geographical isolation, Widmer

Brothers was in a position to do more than just brew and bottle beer. Kurt described the slow, natural process of assimilation between the two companies: "It just evolved that, 'Okay, we'll do your bottles for Hawaii and the mainland.' And then, 'Do you want us to do your draft for the mainland? Do you want to feed into our Anheuser-Busch network? Do you want us to do your sales and marketing on the mainland?' At each step they were like, 'Yeah, that would be great! Yeah, why *wouldn't* we do that?' These were things they couldn't do from Hawaii anyhow, so it was all just a plus for them. Finally it was just, as a separate company this is not making sense anymore, so we blended them in."

Redhook and Widmer Brothers formalized their own merger in 2008, renaming themselves Craft Brewers Alliance. (A few years later they would settle on Craft Brew Alliance.) If joining each other to streamline sales and marketing made sense, then combining operations seemed like a natural next step. Not everyone describes it in exactly these terms, but looking back, Kurt saw it as a natural process akin to the Kona merger. "We were both in the A-B distribution network, so that part was making sense," Kurt said. "But they had a sales guy and we had a sales guy both calling on the exact same wholesalers. So we merged those. And then it was, they had the brewery in Portsmouth and we sent beer all the way across the country—'Can you guys brew for us?' 'Of course.' It just evolved; it was very friendly. It was a win-win. So then it was, let's put these breweries together as one entity. CBA was not some part of a master plan—it just evolved as friends having a beer together."

In 2010, CBA acquired Kona Brewing for $13.9 million. By that time, it was becoming clear that Kona had remarkable potential as a brand, though it still constituted less than a quarter of CBA's sales. In the years since its outright purchase, Kona has tripled in volume, and is now CBA's most valuable brand.

Following the Kona purchase, CBA continued to expand, looking to grow both geographically and across product lines. In April 2012, CBA launched a gluten-free beer line, Omission, which has become a substantial piece of the company. In 2016, Omission alone sold 43,000 barrels—enough to place it in the top seventy largest craft breweries in the United States. A year later, CBA expanded into the growing cider market with Square Mile. Additional affiliations arrived in 2015, when Appalachian Mountain Brewery (Boone, North Carolina) and Cisco Brewers (Nantucket, Massachusetts) were added to the fold. Finally, in 2016, Miami's Wynwood Brewing joined the company.

Through all of this expansion, the Widmer brewery on North Russell Street remained the headquarters of the company. The Widmer brand, however, has seen its place change within Craft Brew Alliance; in fact, Widmer Brothers has almost exactly switched places with Kona. Although Widmer constituted about half the company's sales in 2010, it now accounts for a little over one-fifth of sales. Kona is the company's main driver, selling more than half of CBA's products. It's an entirely different book, but the emergence of Kona is one of the more remarkable success stories in craft brewing. The elegant designs, suffused with the sun and relaxation of the Hawaiian Islands ("Liquid Aloha"), helped attract drinkers to the brand when it first reached the mainland.

In 2016, Craft Brew Alliance's CEO Andy Thomas acknowledged the reality of things when he told Hawaiian journalist Tim Golden, "Kona is the cornerstone of the portfolio now. It's now over 40 percent of our revenue and we believe it's our growth engine for the future." In 2017, CBA announced a plan to build a new 100,000-barrel production facility near the original Kona brewpub in Kailua-Kona.

IN PORTLAND, THERE'S NO "CBA"

As CBA increasingly leans into the Kona brand, what kind of legacy does that leave for Widmer Brothers?

Craft Brew Alliance is a national brewery and one of the biggest beer companies in the country. Widmer Brothers is now a division within the larger company, and no longer its focal point. All of that is true, but in some key ways misleading. Within the Pacific Northwest, Widmer Brothers is very much still a flagship brewery. Based on production, it would still rank as one of the region's top two breweries—bigger than any in Washington State.

In the city of Portland, its relevance is even more significant. Within its hometown, where craft beer is consumed in greater quantity than in any other American city, Widmer is the anchor brewery. When you visit the old brick Smithson and McKay buildings, the sign outside says "Widmer." When you order a beer, the options are all house-brewed Widmer Brothers ales and lagers. If you go to a Blazers or Timbers game, the local beer sponsor is Widmer Brothers. Each autumn, Widmer Brothers hosts a local Oktoberfest. Pretty much anywhere you go in the city, you can find a Widmer Brothers beer. The concept of "Craft Brew Alliance" is only dimly understood around Portland, and there isn't any "CBA" beer. In Portland, the brewery is Widmer, and that's how people understand it.

People who read the beer business news have known about Widmer's changing status within CBA for years. But what many outside Portland fail to understand is what a bedrock institution Widmer Brothers is in its home city. That's not going to change anytime soon. It's something the company has built up over decades, and it's something locals still see—and, when the kettle is boiling away, smell. As long as Widmer Brothers keeps rolling out kegs of fresh Hefeweizen, it's always going to be Portland's city brewery.

THE WIDMER WAY

IN 2005, TWO ORGANIZATIONS REPRESENTING COMMER-
cial breweries—the Association of Brewers and
the Brewers' Association of America—merged to form the
Brewers Association. The new group was created to
promote "craft brewers"—a category that had, at best,
only hazy outlines. The board of directors set about
sharpening those lines and came up with three criteria:
small, traditional, and *independent*. The definition of independent was itself hazy, and as board members tried to
refine it, it became a bone of contention that drove the
organization to a momentous decision.

What constituted independence? Did owners have to
control 100 percent of the company? Where did private
equity fit into the equation? Could "independent" breweries contract brew their beer at an industrial brewery,
as Boston Beer and Pete's Wicked had done, or contract
brew beer *for* industrial breweries, as Full Sail was
doing? As the members hashed out the question, two
elephants loomed in the corner of the room: Redhook
and Widmer. The owners held a controlling majority of

the companies, but Anheuser-Busch—craft brewing's ancient *bête noire*—owned about a third of each. As the Brewers Association board played around with allowable percentages and ownership structures, everyone in the organization knew what the stakes were. Set the line in one place, and these two pioneering breweries would be members in good standing; set it in another, and they would be out of the club.

The board met in 2006 to finalize the guidelines. In order to qualify as "independent," they decided, breweries would have to control 75 percent of the shares of their companies. By the time the meeting ended, Widmer Brothers Brewing Company was out.

THE NATURE OF CRAFT

Ever since Vince Cottone coined the phrase "craft brewery" in 1986, its meaning has been up for debate. Cottone was trying to figure out how to describe the new breweries in his 1986 book, *Good Beer Guide: Breweries and Pubs of the Pacific Northwest*. "I use the term Craft Brewery to describe a small brewery using traditional methods and ingredients to produce a handcrafted, uncompromised beer that is marketed locally," he wrote. (He didn't call the stuff these breweries made "craft beer," opting instead for "true beer." That one never took off.) This definition had its own shortcomings—according to Cottone, Sierra Nevada wouldn't have been a craft brewery by about 1990. But other definitions were equally problematic.

The original Brewers Association definition leaned heavily on the concept of "traditional." There was an idea at the time that national breweries were somehow making a cheater version of beer. It was illegitimate because brewers used the wrong equipment (too big), the wrong ingredients (rice, corn), or the wrong processes (high-gravity brewing). But that meant breweries like Minnesota's Schell's (founded in 1860) and Pennsylvania's Yuengling (1829) weren't traditional. By this definition, a brewery that had been making American lagers the same way for a hundred years was not traditional, but a brewery that started a year ago to make imitations of English ales was. The definition also skirted the issue of contract brewing, which Jim Koch used to launch Boston Beer. Sam Adams was originally brewed by Iron City, and later by Stroh and Heileman.

Indeed, even Cottone's notion of "handcrafted" beer was largely romantic. Brewing is an industrial process, and even small breweries produce remarkably large volumes of beer. By the Brewers Association's current definition, a "microbrewery" may produce up to 15,000 barrels. To most people, that's a meaningless figure, but it amounts to nearly half a million gallons of beer or nearly *five million* bottles. Breweries, even small ones, are factories that churn out beer by the swimming pool. They are all automated to greater or lesser degrees and provide humans little opportunity for handcrafting anything. (And for the people making those millions of gallons, the less handling they have to do, the better.)

But even that doesn't provide the full picture. In brewing, automation amounts to control and precision—two things every brewer wants. The brewing process is long and complex, and if the parameters of each step are variable, it makes it hard for the brewers to make the beer they have in mind. This is why every brewer in the world wants a sophisticated brewery, whether it's 2.5 barrels or 250. As much affection as they may have had for the old dairy equipment brewery on Lovejoy, Kurt and Rob were anxious to move to the larger brewery on Russell Street because it helped them make better beer.

The business of brewing doesn't stop once a brewer hammers the bung into the keg, either. Making the beer is only the first step; getting it to the retailer quickly so every glass is fresh is equally important. The brothers started self-distribution largely out of necessity, but they continued with it long after they grew to a size where most other breweries would have turned to a distributor. Again, the reason was control. They were certain they could do a better job of both delivering fresh beer and helping the pub serve it fresh.

The idea of "craft" can be cut a dozen different ways, but at Widmer Brothers, there was a shorthand for what it meant, internalized to such a degree that many people didn't mention it. Ann Widmer was the first to call the Widmer approach by name. "They have a powerful set of values, which was known as the 'Widmer Way.' It got called that. The Widmer Way was: We don't tell people about products we can't produce. We don't tell distributors we'll give them beer when we're not going to. We don't buy coolers for people even when that would get us the account. We are environmentally sustainable."

The Widmer Way

Rob and Kurt, as leaders of the brewery, had a slightly different orientation to the Widmer Way. They acted as mentors and cheerleaders for their staff. "The Widmer Way was there was no such thing as close enough," Rob said. Thinking of his competitors, he said, "We're just going to outwork them, going to get here earlier, going to stay later, we're going to be better at everything we do, and there isn't such a thing as, 'Oh, it's five,' or 'Close enough,' or any of that. We're just going to outdo them."

Kurt continued: "To Rob's point, I think that's part of the Widmer Way: it's not done until it's done. 'Good enough' and 'close enough'—we told people in the interview process, 'We don't ever want to hear you say that.' We never bark at anybody to hurry—ever. We did tell them repeatedly, 'It's not done until it's done. And if you're not proud of it, it's not done.'" People at the brewery responded to that approach. "Most people want to take pride in their work," Kurt said.

Chad Carbis, who oversaw the self-distribution part of the business, spoke of the Widmer Way most eloquently. "That actually became a huge saying around the brewery," he said. "If any question arose where you said, 'Hey, what should I do here?' Rob would always stop and say, 'Just think of what the Widmer Way is.' And the Widmer

Way was always the best way. The best way to earn trust with the customers, the best way to give the best service, the best quality beer, the honest way. Never cut corners. These were values that were instilled in us every day. It was tough to explain exactly what it was, but when you made a decision, you kind of knew which was the Widmer Way."

The Widmer Way could be considered a holistic approach to craft brewing, encompassing not just the beer, but the internal culture and the way the company interacts with partners and customers. For the first decade of its existence, Widmer Brothers was *the* model craft brewery. That's why the relationship Widmer Brothers forged with Anheuser-Busch was so surprising. They found a kindred spirit in August Busch III, with whom, despite the size of his empire, they had more in common than they did with many other craft breweries. In their respective approaches to brewing, the Widmers and Busch saw eye to eye.

"If you've ever been to an Anheuser-Busch brewery, there's never any wear and tear showing," Kurt said. "Maintenance was a very high priority [for August Busch III]."

Before he'd give his blessing to any relationship with Widmer Brothers, Busch had to personally tour the brewery. What he found when he first visited Portland pleased him enormously. "It was a very well done, *extremely* clean brewery," Busch told me. "They're professionals. They're old-time brewers. You could see that in a heartbeat. They loved their work and they loved their company. They ran their company like we ran ours."

"One time, August asked what our source of CO_2 was," Kurt said when speaking of Busch's commitment to quality. "Sometimes a plant processes urea, and the CO_2 is a byproduct. I was able to tell him that where we get it is a qualified plant and that's all they do. He said, 'Okay, but what about the trucks that deliver it?' I had to say, 'Okay, August, I don't know. I think all they do is CO_2, but I can't tell you.' He told me he was going to send me some background. He sent me—it was a stack like this high—a protocol for CO_2, starting from who makes it and how it's delivered [to] how it's analyzed. I mean, we had never taken a sample of CO_2 here as it came off the truck. We'd never done that—it never even occurred to us. I mean, it's coming from a plant that they already qualified; that this truck might be hauling—I don't know what else a gas truck could be hauling? I'm not kidding, this protocol, it's unbelievable."

Kurt and Rob had different personalities, and no one ever told a story like that about them. (Quite the opposite; their low-key, quiet personalities carried over to their management style.) But that commitment to quality was the same.

The Conscience of the Beer

One of the more surprising discoveries in the Widmer story is the role Rob played at the brewery. He was devoted to the quality of the beer and became the conscience of that quality within the brewery, speaking, as it were, on the beer's behalf. He was one of the champions of the internal tasting panel at the brewery, a critical part of quality assurance. Both Rob and Kurt continue to adore their flagship, but for Rob it has become a lifelong passion. Not only has he pushed the brewery to perfect that beer for over three decades, he even—amazingly—still home-brews Hefeweizen. Below are two anecdotes that illustrate Rob's unique passion.

SEBASTIAN PASTORE: "He was certainly the most involved in tasting beer at Widmer over twenty years. Very, very consistent in that and very, very concerned about it. He was sort of the Jiminy Cricket of the brewery—the conscience of the beer—in that he was always the guy who was the most concerned about the nuances of the flavor of the product. It was a constant theme the entire time that I worked there. Rob's point of view was that it was never good enough until it was perfect, and it was obviously never going to be perfect." He laughed, remembering. "He'd always say, 'Guys, it's just *not quite* ...' We couldn't spend the next two years trying to make the perfect glass of Hefeweizen, but that was really what Rob wanted to do—to spend the next two years trying to make the perfect glass of Hefeweizen."

KURT WIDMER: "Something that Rob would never tell you because he's so modest, but before the Great American Beer Festival ten years ago they did a tasting, twenty-three beers. I don't remember what you were asked to identify—maybe it was the flaw in each one or something like that. One person got twenty-two and nobody else got more than like fifteen. Rob was the one. This was a room of brewers. He's got a really good palate. It's trained, so he has that going for him, too. But nobody else even got close and he almost nailed it, 100 percent. Be forewarned: if you have a beer with Rob, don't ask him what he thinks about the beer because he'll just destroy it for you. Even if you're enjoying it."

Now, let's come back to that concept of "craft." In the course of their evolution, the Widmers focused on decisions that would improve their beer. They made continual technological improvements with each new brewhouse, added a full-scale laboratory to monitor the quality of their beer, and chose the partner with the best distribution network. But their decision to allow Anheuser-Busch to buy a minority stake, a move Widmer Brothers viewed as another improvement to their beer, was seen as decidedly *un*-craft. This had much more to do with the business of beer, however, than the beer itself.

THE "CRAFT" WAR

In the mid- to late 1990s, the antagonism between craft breweries and big breweries—particularly Anheuser-Busch—grew more pointed. When A-B initiated their 100 Percent Share of Mind campaign, craft breweries understood it was targeted directly at them. This was the era when big companies were creating brands that appeared to come from craft breweries (Icehouse and Red Dog from Miller, Red Wolf from Anheuser-Busch, Blue Moon from Coors), but were merely specialty divisions inside the giants. Among craft brewers, these felt like aggressive responses targeted at their businesses.

In retaliation, Boston Beer's Jim Koch spearheaded a counterattack. He questioned the quality of mass-market lagers and claimed they included preservatives. Responding to the stealth craft labels the big breweries had created, Boston Beer petitioned the government to require breweries to list where the beer had been made. Mitch Steele, the brewer then working in the new products division at Anheuser-Busch, described how that went down in St. Louis: "In trying to create some separation between what he was brewing and what the bigger companies were brewing, he talked a lot about the use of adjuncts and how evil that was. And [Koch mentioned] the use of preservatives—which Anheuser-Busch never even used—but Jim Koch certainly implied that Anheuser-Busch used preservatives. It just *infuriated* August Busch."

Of course, this caused A-B to retaliate. Anheuser-Busch responded by targeting the contract-brewing element of Boston Beer, even getting a major news story placed on NBC's *Dateline* that ran like an indictment. This time, Koch was incensed. The punches flew back and forth.

This polarization created a new consciousness around craft brewing (a term that was slowly supplanting "microbrewing"). A kind of morality developed: craft was on the side of goodness, quality, and harmony, while big breweries were bad, cheap, and destructive. Anheuser-Busch was no longer dangerous just because of its competitive advantage—it was actively trying to crush craft breweries. The industry friction was exacerbated by the slowdown in craft sales, which flattened between 1995 and the early 2000s.

To be clear, Anheuser-Busch *was* a real threat to craft brewing. Mitch Steele, tasked with creating beers inside the brewery to compete with craft, saw the turbulence craft was creating within the company. After developing a craft-type ale, Steele recalls, "A guy pulled me out the meeting and goes, 'You know, we don't want to grow this category; we want to [get] to the point where our beers take over and the rest of them go away.'" Even Widmer CEO Terry Michaelson acknowledged the dynamic. "Certainly A-B did a lot of things; they tried scorched earth, they tried to keep people out of their wholesalers, and so there were a lot of reasons for small brewers to not like what A-B was doing."

As a consequence, anyone associated with Anheuser-Busch was highly suspicious to other craft breweries. Prior to Widmer Brothers' excommunication from the Brewers Association, other craft breweries started to wonder if the Widmers were acting as a mole within the community, reporting their secrets back to Anheuser-Busch. "There was already the concern that we may be an A-B spy," Michaelson recalled. "For a long time, A-B paranoia really fueled what was happening with that group."

With their ejection from the ranks of "craft brewers," an interesting thing happened in their home market. For a decade, Widmer Brothers had taken heat for their involvement with Anheuser-Busch, but no one seriously thought the brewery was a front for St. Louis. When the Brewers Association ejected the brewery, there was something like a family reaction—"Hey, *I* can pick on my little brother, but you better leave him alone." All of this happened just after Widmer Brothers' twentieth anniversary, and locals began taking an inventory of the company's actions around town.

For years, the Widmers had quietly run laboratory analyses for any brewery that asked. "We never told anybody about anybody else's findings or anything like that," Kurt said. "We never charged a dime for it. And you know, for a while I resented the fact that they would come in the dead of night and there would be a trap door that would open up and they'd hand the sample in and our guys would do the analysis and hand it back and nobody would ever know. But I get that." Most smaller breweries don't have a full lab, the kind that can give accurate measures of bitterness, and the Widmers were happy to test samples—and do to this day.

Widmer Brothers also sponsored a project, one that continues to this day, with a local homebrew club called the Collaborator Program. Each year, the club holds a competition, and the winning beers are brewed throughout the year by Widmer and released commercially. One or two have become so popular they've gotten a general Widmer release. In 2017, the club awarded Rob Widmer the "Collaborator Bung," a kind of lifetime achievement award for championing the program.

Perhaps most importantly, the Widmers were just good members of the brewing community. I recall a time in 2011 when I was at Breakside, then a small three-barrel brewpub in Northeast Portland that had been around about a year. The brewer, Ben Edmunds, was working on a gose—a mostly extinct sour ale originally from Leipzig. Ben had wanted to see how other breweries made the beer, so he asked to see the process and formulation other brewers had used. This isn't always typical, but it is in Portland, where information is pretty freely shared among breweries. Ben pulled up the emails he'd gotten. One was from Upright, another small brewery, and one was from Widmer Brothers. Both sent along every detail about the recipes and formulation.

By 2006, consumers had spent more than twenty years drinking craft beer. They understood what it was. There was a collective snort across Beervana when the Brewers Association—an organization in Colorado—decided it would dictate which breweries were and weren't craft breweries. In Portland, even critics of Widmer Brothers had a hard time swallowing the notion that they weren't "craft." There they were, scenting Russell Street with boiling wort, as they had been for years. To many people who had been drinking this beer for decades, Kurt and Rob were as craft as it got.

It has now been decades since small breweries started repopulating the cities and small towns in America. When they began, the United States had fewer breweries than at any time since the eighteenth century. Those few decades have seen a complete reversal, and there are now more breweries than at any time in history. Over those few decades, what Americans think of as "good" beer has changed many times. We've associated quality with brewery size, ingredients, ownership, and indefinable notions of aesthetics. As the new century grows longer in the tooth, trying to define "good" or "craft" becomes ever more elusive. For the Widmers—and probably every brewery—the standards were the ones they used in-house. The "Widmer Way" didn't map to any definitions of craft brewing, but it was the fundamental value that guided the brewery. If people want to understand what unites the actions Rob and Kurt took, from the time they dumped their first ten batches of beer to the moment they signed with Anheuser-Busch, it can be found in the values embodied in that shorthand phrase.

A LEGACY OF BEER

ONE OF THE MOST COMMONLY TOLD ANECDOTES about Kurt and Rob is at once revealing and inscrutable. Back in the days at Lovejoy, the two brothers shared an office. When they moved to Russell Street, they continued the practice, but to the surprise and fascination of onlookers, placed their desks so that they faced each other. Rob's wife, Barb Widmer, marveled at this. "You know what, if my brother or sister and I sat across the desk from each other, we wouldn't have made it two days." But she also saw the desk arrangement as a pointed example of their working relationship; it explained something essential about the brothers. "They were a complement to each other. Kurt is more the intellectual; Rob is more the 'I can do that.' As adults, they always got along and they could agree to disagree. Their relationship is special."

To Sebastian Pastore, the arrangement shone a light on something very brotherly. "Kurt was always the older brother and acted like the older brother. And Rob was always the younger brother and deferred to the older brother." They were able to work together so well because

Kurt and Rob's first office at the brewery on Lovejoy, which they called "The Situation Room."

they didn't vie for control. Kurt was the executive, "the boss," and Rob focused on "the beer, the brewing; he took an early interest in quality."

When Terry Michaelson joined the company as CEO, he got a front row seat to this unusual desk arrangement. "For the first three months, the upstairs wasn't built—where I would have my office. I sat in what we refer to as the training desk." His desk was a smaller one, off to the side, and in a different environment, this might have been considered a slight or power play. Looking back, though, Terry felt fortunate to have seen them working together while he absorbed information about the business by being in the middle of things. "I listened to them talk about the industry and go back and forth. It was an amazing period."

For the people who commented on it, the office arrangement was a visible symbol of how well Kurt and Rob worked together—that the brewery was very much headed by a two-man team. But *how* they could manage to exist in such close proximity for so long, and *why* they would want to—these questions were left unanswered. This turned out to be a central fact of the story: Kurt and Rob do not easily reveal themselves. As various people unfolded their versions of the Widmer story, they focused on events more than the motivations and personalities of the founders. People were reluctant to speculate about the interior lives of the Widmer brothers because, even after decades, they have revealed so little of themselves.

Many companies are headed and ultimately defined by the gregarious, larger-than-life personalities of their founders. In companies like Apple, Berkshire Hathaway, or Tesla, it's hard to know where the CEO ends and the company begins. With Widmer Brothers, that relationship exists—profoundly, in fact—but is much less direct. People reach for the desk anecdote because it reveals the distinctive, if elusive, personalities that were at the heart of the brewery. Looking back over the key elements of the Widmer story, certain themes emerge: the let's-do-it-ourselves ethos of self-distribution, the emphasis on building relationships pub by pub, the focus on quality that led them to dump early batches of beer, the desire to have their beer speak for itself rather than making a brand of their personalities. The Widmer Way. And all of these go back to the quiet yet insistent personalities of those two men sitting at desks across from each other.

PRIVATE LIVES

To prepare for this book, I interviewed Rob and Kurt over the course of about ten hours. For the first two or three sessions, I kept waiting for the men to reveal their internal experiences of the past thirty-five years, to express what it felt like at each critical moment. When I asked them to recall how something felt, they would struggle to describe it using those terms. Instead, they'd tell me what happened.

An example: one of the more painful moments came after Widmer Brothers announced its partnership with Anheuser-Busch. As a reaction to what some people felt was a betrayal, false rumors started proliferating about the brewery. One story was common enough that Widmer had to respond: a story circulated that Hefeweizen contained a thousand calories. "I mean, think about it: a *milkshake* doesn't have a thousand calories in it," Rob said. "We had it analyzed and put it on a point-of-sale sheet. But you know, the deal with A-B, we'd sold out, so we didn't have any credibility." They suspected it was started by a competitor and was kept alive by people who wanted to see something nefarious in Widmer's success.

I asked how this felt. In reply, they gave me five separate anecdotes about the ways in which the A-B deal had helped them make better beer. (They were good ones, too, all five appearing somewhere in this book.)

For the Widmers, this story wasn't about feelings; it was about the incongruity between the way their beer had improved as a result of the A-B partnership and the way people assumed it had actually made it worse. I could infer how it must have felt, but it's not the way they related to that experience.

About halfway through our interviews, it dawned on me. Rob and Kurt weren't failing to reveal themselves with these answers; they were being totally transparent. It's just that they don't process things by thinking about how they made them *feel*; they channel that energy into troubleshooting and figuring out solutions. This was as much the case with their triumphs, too. When I asked about the meteoric success of Hefeweizen or the attention they attracted from potential suitors, they would answer with anecdotes about how they responded to these events.

A nearly universal theme among the people I spoke to for this book was how private Kurt and Rob are. Most people characterized it as a positive for the business because it created a low-key, collegial environment. But it presented certain challenges, too. Rob and Kurt's name was on the label, and not just their family name—the two brothers. They were literally the faces of the brewery. In terms of branding, that meant thrusting the brothers into the public eye. Some of the brewing pioneers, like Boston Beer's Jim Koch, Dogfish Head's Sam Calagione, or Brooklyn Brewing's Garrett Oliver, are gregarious and comfortable in front of a microphone. They have been quoted hundreds or thousands of times. Some have had their own television shows; all appear regularly on television, and all have published books.

The Widmer brothers are far less comfortable playing that role. "They became very much the face of the brand, and sometimes that was uncomfortable for them," Tim McFall, the marketing director, remembered. "They didn't necessarily want to be that prominent and well-known, but they also understood that they were the brand. They were always good sports about it, but I know there was a period there where they were unsure as to how their private personalities and public personalities meshed or not."

By contrast, they were completely happy to be the face of the brewery on a more intimate level. If McFall wanted them to visit a new state Widmer was trying to enter, that was no problem. "They would be out in the grocery stores doing the sampling. They would go to a marketplace and hook up with a sales guy in, say, Arizona, and Kurt or Rob would go store to store or bar to bar talking to people." Of course, when they did this, they often failed to tell the shopper tasting their beer that they were one of the guys on the bottle.

Being good in front of a camera requires comfort with self-revelation (whether play-acted or real), so it's no surprise the Widmers found it challenging. For Rob and Kurt, the point of focus was the beer itself, or the work needed to make it and get it into the hands of customers. From their perspective, this didn't require emotional demonstrations. Pastore put it bluntly: for the Widmers, "it was just work, work, work, work, work."

For those who looked closely, their reserve was evidence of a remarkable level of loyalty and trust. This was the way the brothers tried to convey their connection and commitment to their staff. Pastore, who had no brewing experience when he started as a fresh college graduate in the 1980s, noticed the way he was treated as an equal. "Kurt and Rob were very much egalitarian, of-the-people type people. One of the things that was interesting about the early days at Widmer is that everybody's business card said 'Brewer.' I don't think Kurt was ever that comfortable being a big executive, the CEO; I've never seen him in a suit. Neither one of them was ever fancy."

Widmer employees talked a lot about how hard the work was at Widmer, and how high the expectations were. This ethos was forged in the early days, when the work was back-breaking and everyone was expected to pitch in. "The thing I remember about the early days?" Chad Carbis, who would go on to head self-distribution, described the situation: "We didn't have a forklift. So we lifted everything, literally by hand. Same thing with the grain truck. We didn't have silos; it was all 50-pound sacks and we'd have to chain-gang 'em into the brewery and stack 'em by hand." Yet the brothers didn't stand back and bark out orders—they lifted and toted and stacked right along with everyone else. More than a few people said this made working with them, and Ray in the early days, feel like a part of the family.

This manifested in other ways, too. Once they handed off a job, the Widmers assumed it would get done, and get done right. Employees were also empowered to defend their positions as experts in their fields. McFall told a revealing story about how this led to conflict. "Sometimes our ideas were different. I remember distinctly one time [Kurt] and I were really heated on something. I told him, I said, 'Listen, Kurt, I get it. I absolutely get it. I know what you built and I know how important it is to you, and the day that I stop battling you on these things, fighting for what I believe in with you, is the day that I'm done here.' And he respected that. But that's the relationship we had. He allowed his people a ton of autonomy."

When Kurt and Rob decided to bring in a new CEO to run the business, it could have sparked a battle of wills. Yet Terry Michaelson said the opposite happened. "They trusted me with some humongous decisions that had a big impact on what happened. There wasn't a decision being made without them saying yes, but [they allowed] the team to do the analysis and come to them and say, 'Okay, here's what it looks like and here's what we think should happen.'"

In some cases, their private personalities could be misinterpreted, too. Angel Marquez came to the brewery as a teenager in the 1980s. "I've known them most of my life; they were prominent male figures in my life, in my childhood, even," he said. Yet at work, Marquez never felt he got to know either boss. "Bumping into Kurt and Rob in the break room and the hallway, I always get the impression that they're in a hurry to go somewhere else. If I start to try to chat them up, Kurt looks like he needs to go. So I break it off as quickly as convenient and let it go."

Yet Marquez mentioned this in the context of a revelation he'd recently had about the brothers. In July 2015, a driver had a seizure while turning onto Russell Street right in front of the brewery. Marquez was walking between two of the buildings when the car struck him from behind. It was a very serious accident, causing extensive damage to his back and head, and required a lengthy convalescence, including long hospital stays.

"Kurt and Rob were there almost every day," he said. "I was *stunned*. I was stunned. You know, as much distance as you guys have kept with me all these years, now you're here every day. It's really great to see you guys! It was very interesting to have them come visit me in the hospital every day. I couldn't get out of the bed, and when I could I needed a walker—and they would still show up. I couldn't interact with them very much, but they would still show up. Almost every single day, even when they transferred me to a brain injury recovery clinic in another hospital, they would still show up. And then after I go home, I can't go to work, I can't drive, but they still want to have lunch with me. These guys got big hearts, they really do."

ANN AND BARB ON KURT AND ROB

Among all the people I spoke to over the course of this project, there were two who would not describe Rob and Kurt as inscrutable—Barb and Ann Widmer, the women who were with them through the decades of this adventure. As we neared the end of our conversations about the men, I asked about who they are as people, outside the brewhouse.

Kurt met Ann in 1980. She had children from another marriage, and Kurt helped her raise them. Rob and Barb met in 1992 and were married a couple years later. Both couples live in modest homes they've owned for decades in the same part of Southwest Portland. Neither family has a taste for luxury items or cars. As with their work lives, their home lives are low-key and without ostentation. Not long ago, reporters following craft brewing calculated that, at least in terms of their assets, Sierra Nevada's Ken Grossman and Boston Beer's Jim Koch were billionaires. But the two brothers from a lower middle-class Portland background have continued to live quiet, modest lives despite their brewing successes.

Ann and Barb on Kurt and Rob

BARB: "Rob still likes to have—he's a hands-on guy. He's like his dad. His dad was a fix-it guy, he was a tractor salesman ... Rob is in many ways that same fix-it guy. He loves YouTube because he can figure out how to fix almost anything. He's waiting for his iPhone battery to die, because he's going to change it. Can't be done, right? He is dying to do it."

ANN: "Kurt loves to read. He's an avid reader. He reads *hours* every day. He reads a lot of things that I would call high-level fiction—not murder mysteries and the stuff people read on airplanes. In the morning he reads the *New York Times*, the *Wall Street Journal*, and *The Oregonian*—and that's by nine o'clock. He just read *All the Light We Cannot See*. We belong to Portland Literary Arts and go to the lectures, their series."

BARB: "I said, 'What are you going to do when you retire?' He said, 'I'm going to have to take up a hobby.' It's not like he's going to be cleaning the house. He really likes cars and stuff like that, but his big thing is he wants to backpack the Pacific Crest Trail if his body holds up. We did Oregon together."

ANN: "He did drive a car for a while out at the track. He had a little Porsche 911—an old Porsche, not an expensive one. He drove that for a while and he was a very good driver. He got really busy at the brewery—the last CBA years were really busy—and he kind of backed away from that."

BARB: "I've seen Rob mad once; he kicked our barbecue. We just have a little tiny barbecue. It wouldn't light, and he kicked it. That's the only time I've seen him get pissed. Every once in a while I bring it up. 'Remember when you kicked the barbecue and I laughed?' It amuses him. He'll get worked up about things, but the only time I've ever seen him get mad."

ANN: "He's an honest, straightforward—this kind of brings tears to my eyes. He's a hard worker. He's critical. He is stubborn to some extent, which kind of goes with that steadfast thing and that strong thing. He's as good as his word."

BARB: "He really is the kindest person I've ever known. The most recent example: we have this habit of noticing homeless people in the neighborhood. A few years ago there was a gal, we thought she was living in her truck in the neighborhood. So we started leaving things on her truck. Now we have her over for Christmas and stuff like that. Now he's noticed this one guy, his name's Wade, and he's seen him for a few years and he's started to get to know him. Every morning he tries to drop some stuff off with him. He's so funny: 'Every day I get a little bit more.' He's been on the street for thirty years. Rob will be looking at his iPad and say, 'I can't get my mind off Wade.'"

ANN: "He's also been pretty good at letting me be me. I had a substantive career before I met Kurt and he's encouraged me to continue that. Everybody assumed I'd retire when Kurt retired, but he retired kind of early for my perspective. I remember the moment. He came home and I was in the driveway weeding some hydrangeas and he said, 'I'm going to retire.' It freaked me out because I wasn't ready to retire—but he said, 'That's okay.'"

Near the very end of our conversation, Barb mentioned another anecdote she's seen play out many times in their decades together. The story is specifically about Rob, but encapsulates both brothers' approach to owning a brewery.

"So this is what Rob does," she began. "We may go out for a beer. If we see someone else at another table drinking a Widmer Hefeweizen, he'll introduce himself to the bartender and say, 'Hi, I'm Rob Widmer, I'd love to buy that person that beer.' And he [has] a little sticker. Each time we pay our bill, he puts this little 'Thanks for pouring Widmer' sticker on the bill. Even if we're in Jolly Roger's, right down the street from us. He still puts it on every time. And he tries to make connections with people. Not just the bartender, but people."

PORTLAND'S BREWERY

If you wanted to somehow characterize Kurt and Rob's legacy, walking around their brewery is not a bad place to start. Before I finished interviewing them, I did just that, letting them act as tour guides. Words are great, but the physical environment of a brewery—the sounds, smells, and sights—communicates in a more visceral way.

I've also discovered that polished stainless steel has a way of eliciting stories one forgets when working with memory alone. Sometimes a random fact leads to a great anecdote. For example, the brewery recently installed an in-line scale for their grain, a detail that emerged as we visited the barley mill near the start of the tour. The device allows brewers to weigh the malt as it passes from the grain silo on its way to the mill. "We're going to get rid of the weighing hopper, so it's not filling the hopper and dumping it—it's just as fast as the malt can go," Rob explained.

There's a pragmatic purpose behind this gee-whiz tech: an in-line scale speeds up the process sufficiently enough for the brewery to do twelve brews a day instead of ten. As we walked a little farther, that fact reminded Rob of a day over thirty years earlier. "The very first time we did two batches in a day—because clean-up, I forget how many hours, but it was like half the day. It was climbing in; it was really hot, dirty, and physical, all that. And to get twice as much beer for the same effort, it was like, 'This is awesome.'"

Touring a brewery brings home the reality of just how much beer it makes. Widmer Brothers uses an average of 75,000 pounds of wheat a week—about four million pounds a year. And that's just wheat; the amount of barley is even larger. Silos standing outside the brewery can hold up to 100,000 pounds of grain, which seems like a staggering amount until you realize that tens of thousands of pounds go through the brewery every day. "There's either a truck there waiting for spent grain or a truck delivering new grain," Kurt said.

When we arrived at the fermentation cellars, the gallons of beer produced by those pounds of malt become visible in the grandeur of the tanks, which reach up four stories high. "They're the largest tanks that can be sent over the interstate highway system," Rob said as we craned our necks to see the top. Later, as robotic arms effortlessly hoisted kegs of beer and stacked them for shipping, Kurt explained that the adjacent line fills 520 bottles a minute—more than eight bottles every second.

Each year, the Oregon Brewers Guild calculates all the people associated with the brewing industry, looking at

Kurt and Rob celebrating the 30th anniversary of Widmer Brothers.

workers who deliver the beer, grow the hops, and make the brewing equipment. More than three people are supported by the brewing industry for every one that works in it directly. "Our wheat," Kurt said, "is grown mostly in Oregon and Washington, Idaho, Western Montana—same as our barley." An acre produces about 2,500 pounds of wheat, which means Widmer Brothers requires farmers to tend around 12,000 acres for that grain alone. Then it must be harvested, delivered, and malted, employing more people along the way before it ever reaches North Russell Street.

The brewery grows every year, but it's been big for a long time. In the mid-1980s, the local malthouse in Vancouver, Washington, didn't offer malted wheat, so Rob and Kurt had to order it from Wisconsin. "We were taking entire truckloads of wheat malt, but it was still expensive to ship it across the country. Great Western in Vancouver started malting wheat when our volumes got to the point where it made sense. We went from a couple tons of wheat the first year to, I don't know, hundreds of tons."

To stand in the brewery is to appreciate the size of Kurt and Rob Widmer's accomplishments. I started adding up the number of bottles the brewery uses each year (well over a hundred and fifty million), the pounds of hops (over a million), the gallons of water (twenty-two million), the drums of ink used to color the labels (incalculable), and on and on. Seeing it all brings home the full, tangible measure of the brewery. It is a *gigantic* enterprise.

This doesn't, however, capture the Widmers' less tangible but perhaps more indelible legacy. They introduced one of the country's most important ales, helping create the mold for what "American" beer should taste like. As founders of craft brewing, they own some part of the credit for changing the way Americans relate to beer. Had Kurt and Rob gone into banking or coffee instead, craft beer would still have flourished in the United States, but its character would have been different. Only a few breweries have had as much impact.

And as is the way of larger, established breweries, their legacy exists in the collective consciousness of the city of Portland. Over time, the character of a town and the character of a brewery start to reflect each other so that it's impossible to imagine them separated. Dublin has Guinness, Copenhagen has Carlsberg, London has Fuller's, Munich has Paulaner and Spaten.

Portlanders will immediately recognize this because their town has already experienced this phenomenon. The Blitz-Weinhard brewery, the husk of which still stands on West Burnside Street in downtown Portland, closed in 1999. Henry Weinhard himself, the founder, died in 1904. And yet, if you stopped to ask a Portlander to tell you the story of the Skidmore Fountain, they'll probably be quick with the answer. In 1888, Henry offered to pump beer through the fountain for the grand opening. City leaders, fearing mayhem, politely declined. Next to the story about how Asa Lovejoy and Francis Pettygrove flipped a coin over naming rights to the city, it may be the most famous Portland anecdote. Portlanders who lived in the city up until Blitz-Weinhard's closure remember how the big brewery dominated and scented downtown with its soothing, burbling presence.

The amount of beer coming out of the Widmer Brothers brewery is not quite as large as Henry's was during its heyday, and Henry's sat on Burnside Street for 143 years before it closed, so it had an extra century to be sewn into the fabric of the city. Nevertheless, the most important legacy of the Widmers, one that grows with each bubbling batch that scents North Russell Street, is the way it becomes more and more firmly a defining piece of the city. It's not possible to imagine Portland without its rose gardens, its rivers and bridges, its shipyards or fir-covered parks or cloudy skies. And with each year that passes, it's harder and harder to think of a Portland without Widmer Brothers. Rob and Kurt helped create craft beer in America, introduced a classic beer, and helped turn Portland into Beervana.

ABOUT THE AUTHOR

Photo by Sadie Verville

THE WIDMER BROTHERS/CRAFT BREW ALLIANCE HIRED award-winning and local Portland writer of all things beer, Jeff Alworth, to write their biography. Alworth has written several beer books, including *The Beer Bible* and *Secrets of Master Brewers: The Traditions & Techniques of the World's Classic Beer Styles*. He has a beer blog, on which he posts weekly, and co-hosts the *Beervana* podcast with Oregon State University economics professor Patrick Emerson.

OOLIGAN PRESS

OOLIGAN PRESS IS A STUDENT-RUN PUBLISHING HOUSE rooted in the rich literary culture of the Pacific Northwest. Founded in 2001 as part of Portland State University's Department of English, Ooligan is dedicated to the art and craft of publishing. Students pursuing master's degrees in book publishing staff the press in an apprenticeship program under the guidance of a core faculty of publishing professionals.

PROJECT MANAGERS
T. J. Carter
Kelly Hogan

PROJECT TEAM
Jessica DeBolt
Sanjay Dharawat
Brittney Finato
Stephen Hyde
Julie Lawson
Olivia Rollins
Hazel Wright
Hanna Ziegler

ACQUISITIONS
Alyssa Schaffer
Joanna Szabo

EDITING
Lisa Hein
Hilary Louth
Emma Hovley
Madison Schultz
Kaitlin Barnes
T. J. Carter
Brittney Finato
Michele Ford
Des Hewson
Elise Hitchings
Kelly Hogan

Megan Huddleston
Kristen Ludwigsen
Meagan Nolan
Tori Raible
Alyssa Schaffer
Monique Vieu
P.J. Zettle

DESIGN
Andrea McDonald
Jenny Kimura
Hanna Ziegler

DIGITAL
Stephanie Argy
Kaitlin Barnes

MARKETING
Morgan Nicholson
Sydney Kiest

SOCIAL MEDIA
Katie Fairchild
Sadie Verville

INDEX

Barley Mill, 89

bartenders, 89

beer culture, 10–12, 55–58, 74–75

Beer of the Year (Fred Eckhardt), 68

Beervana, 91, 188–190

Belmont Inn, 89

Bend, Oregon, 29–30

Bern, Switzerland, 21

Bernau, Jim, 94, 122

Big Sky, Montana, 13

bitterbier, 31

bitterness, 67–68, 169

Black Butte Porter (Deschutes Brewery), 29–30

Blazers, Portland Trail, 157

Blitz–Weinhard, 12, 25, 68, 100, 117, 189

Blue Moon (Coors), 167

Boston Beer, 29, 46, 143, 158, 167, 176, 181

Boston Lager (Boston Beer), 29, 91

bottled beer, 15, 57–58, 94, 116–117, 121–122

bottling, 15, 42, 49–50, 55, 110, 130, 138–141, 148, 153, 186

Bowman, Fred, 57

branding, 72, 109, 113–115, 137–138, 141, 176

Breakside, 170

brew sheets, 82–83

breweries, the Great Recession and, 58

Brewers Association, 118, 158–160, 168–169, 170

Brewers' Association of America, 158

brewpubs, 30, 57, 60–61, 99–101, 104,

BridgePort, 2, 12, 15, 38, 57, 60, 62, 66, 92, 94

D

dairy equipment, 26, 33–34, 106, 161

Dateline, 167

Datsun, 18, 61, 100

Desai Capital Management, 127

Deschutes Brewery, 29–32, 91

designated drinkers, 68

distribution, 59–64, 117, 127–128, 133–134, 140, 150–152, 161

Dogfish Head Brewery, 46, 176

draft, 55, 57–58, 61, 116, 121

dry hopping, 37

Dublin Pub, 81, 84–85, 88–89

Düsseldorf, Germany, 21, 30–32, 50, 72, 75

Duvel Moortgat, 152

E

Eckhardt, Fred, 68, 92

Edmunds, Ben, 170

electric blankets, 39, 47

Engele, Emma, 9–10, 22–23

equipment, 16, 26–28, 31–43, 48, 106

ESB (strong English bitter), 29

F

F. H. Steinbart (homebrew store), 13

Fargo, North Dakota, 22–23

fermentation, 36–37, 79, 124

fermenters, 37, 39, 81

filters, 38–39, 103

filtration, 72, 81, 85

financing, 2, 17–20, 116, 117–121, 126–127

Fish, Gary, 29–30

Freiburg, Germany, 10–11

Fuggle (hop), 80

G

Gambrinus, 152

Garvey, Mark, 124

Germany, 3–4, 7, 10–12, 14, 21, 30–32, 35, 50, 67, 72, 75, 79–80, 86, 170, 189

gluten–free beer, 155

Golden, Tim, 156

Good Beer Guide: Breweries and Pubs of the Pacific Northwest, 159–160

Goose Hollow Inn tavern, 56

Goose Island Beer Company, 151–153

gose, 170

Grant's, 16

Great American Beer Festival, 165–166

Great Recession, the, 58

Great Western, 12, 40, 188

Grossman, Ken, 125, 181

H

Hair of the Dog, 113

Hall, John, 152

Hawaii, 153–154, 156

haze, 38, 72, 80–81, 84–85, 96–97, 138

Healy, Cameron, 153

Heathman Group, 99, 101

hefeweizen, 94, 115

Hefeweizen (Widmer), 73, 74, 80–89, 91–94, 96–98,
    100, 101, 102, 115, 122, 138, 157, 165, 175, 184
    bottling of, 138

Heidelberg, 12

Heileman, 126, 137, 160

Heineken, 68, 136

Henzi, Walter, 6, 9, 13

Heppner, Oregon, 87

Hieronymus, Stan, 97

Higgins, Greg, 99

homebrewing, 6, 9–10, 13–14

hop jacks, 79

hops, 14, 36–37, 68, 79–80, 86, 96, 97, 188

Horse Brass, 89

hot side, 36

Huppmann, 124–125

I

Icehouse (Miller), 167

independence, definitions of, 158–159

infusion mashing, 35

ingenuity, 35–36, 38–43

Iron City, 160

Ivancie, Frank, 56

K

Kalama, Washington, 93

keg-filler, Ray Widmer's, 42–43

kettle, 15, 32, 36, 37, 75, 157
Koch, Jim, 29–30, 160, 167, 176, 181
kölsch, 3–4, 31, 75
Kona Brewing, 153–156

L

lagers, 30–31, 36, 37, 51
Lagunitas, 136
Larrance, Art, 57
lauter, 37
Leipzig, Germany, 170
lemon, 84, 86–87
Literary Arts, 182
localism, 53–58
Lombard Street, 56
Louis the XIV (tavern), 50, 62–63
Lucky·Lager, 12

M

Maletis, Rob, 136
Maletis Beverage, 135–136
Marquez, Angel, 41–42, 45, 46–47, 111, 138, 179–180
Marshall High School (Portland), 7
mash, 37
mash schedules, 78–79
mash tuns, 14, 26, 34–36, 37, 62, 138
mass–market lagers, 51, 66–67, 153
Master Distribution Agreement, 150
McFall, Tim, 113–114, 139, 177, 179
McMenamin, Brian, 57, 58, 60

McMenamin, Mike, 57, 58, 60

McMenamins, 57, 58, 60

Michaelson, Terry, 111–113, 114–115, 123–124, 126, 130–131, 140, 141–142, 148–149, 151, 168, 173, 179

Miller, Morgan, 89

Miller Brewing Company, 115, 116, 126, 127, 131, 167

Modern Brewer, 123

movie theaters, 1, 55

Munich, Germany, 32, 189

N

National Register of Historic Places, 103

New York Times, 94, 182

North Dakota, 22–23

Nor'Wester Brewery, 94, 115, 122

Not So Professional Beer Blog, 93

O

Ockert, Karl, 12, 38, 57, 94

Oktoberfest (Widmer Brothers), 157

Oliver, Garrett, 94, 176

Olympia Brewing Company, 12, 26

Omission Brewing, 155

100 Percent Share of Mind (Anheuser–Busch), 135, 166

Oregon, 1, 7–8, 11–12, 15, 21, 51–55, 59–60, 74, 78, 89, 91, 94, 96–97, 143, 187

Oregon Ale and Beer Company (Boston Beer), 143

Oregon Brewers Festival, 48

Oregon Brewers Guild, 186

Oregon State University, 7

Pyramid, 93–94, 115, 139

Pyramid Hefeweizen, 94

Q

quality, 26, 36, 38, 49–50, 75, 96–98, 118, 129, 133, 140,
162–166, 171, 173

R

Rainier Brewing Company, 12

Ramsay, Stuart, 53–54, 92

Raspberry Weizen (Nor'Wester Brewery), 94

recipe sheets, 76–77

Red Dog (Miller), 167

Red Wolf (Anheuser-Busch), 167

Reddy, Sanjay, 93

Redhook Brewery, 16, 29, 115, 125, 127–128, 135, 137, 145,
147, 149, 151–152, 154, 158

Reed College, 42, 107

regulations, 59–60

Romain, Paul, 59–60

Rusty Pelican, 69

Rymeski, Jay, 26

S

Samuel Adams (Boston Beer), 29, 91

scaling, 119–122, 122–125, 144

Scappoose, Oregon, 21

Schell's, 160

Schlüssel (brewery), 31

Schnitzler, Josef, 31–32

Turnsten, Steve, 78

U

V

W

Willamette Week, 3, 91, 92

wort, 32, 36–37, 39, 79, 170

Wynwood Brewing, 155

Y

Yaeger, Brian, 92

Yakima, Washington, 12

yeast, 14, 30, 32, 34, 36, 37, 39, 72, 78

Yuengling, 160

Z

Ziemann, 124–125

Zum Uerige, 31–32, 34, 35